THE KIDS'
WORLD ALMANAC® OF
BASEBALL

THE KIDS'
WORLD ALMANAC® OF
BASEBALL

THOMAS G. AYLESWORTH

Illustrated by John Lane
Introduction by Cal Ripken, Jr.

WORLD ALMANAC
AN IMPRINT OF PHAROS BOOKS • A SCRIPPS HOWARD COMPANY

NEW YORK

Trademarks appearing on pages 125 through 135 are reprinted with permission from Major League Baseball Properties, Inc. 1990.

Photos used for illustrations on pages 58 through 90: Babe Ruth and Rollie Fingers by permission of the National Baseball Library; Roger Maris, Mickey Mantle, and Joe DiMaggio courtesy The New York Yankees; Frank Robinson courtesy Baltimore Orioles; Roberto Clemente courtesy Pittsburgh Pirates; Carl Yastrzemski courtesy Boston Red Sox; Juan Marichal courtesy San Francisco Giants; Stan Musial courtesy St. Louis Cardinals; Sandy Koufax by permission of Los Angeles Dodgers; Luis Aparicio and Johnny Bench, AP/Wide World; and from NEA/Acme Hank Aaron, Luke Appling, Lou Boudreau, Mordecai Brown, Roy Campanella, Ty Cobb, Dizzy Dean, Bob Feller, Lou Gehrig, Ferguson Jenkins, Harmon Killebrew, Connie Mack, Willie Mays, Satchel Paige, Cal Ripken, Jr., Jackie Robinson, Tom Seaver, Warren Spahn, Casey Stengel, and Cy Young.

First published in 1990.

Library of Congress Cataloging-in-Publication Data

Aylesworth, Thomas G.
  The kids world almanac of baseball / by Thomas G. Aylesworth ; introduction by Cal Ripken, Jr. — Rev. ed.
    p. cm.
  Includes index.
  ISBN 0-88687-721-0
  1. Baseball—United States—Miscellanea—Juvenile literature.
  I. Title.
GV867.3.A97   1993
796.357′0973—dc20   92-35867
                                                             CIP
                                                              AC

Pharos Books are available at special discounts on bulk purchases for sales promotions, premiums, fundraising or educational use. For details, contact Special Sales Department, Pharos Books, 200 Park Avenue, New York, NY 10166.

Printed in the United States of America

Cover design by Sara Stemen
Text design by Bea Jackson
Interior illustrations by John Lane

World Almanac
An Imprint of Pharos Books
A Scripps Howard Company
New York, NY 10166

10 9 8 7 6 5 4 3 2 1

This book is dedicated to Wrigley Field
before the lights were installed.

THOMAS G. AYLESWORTH is the author of ninety-four books. During his tenure as senior editor and editor-in-chief of two major publishing houses, he has edited numerous sports books. In addition, he has written and edited many sports articles, beginning with his role as sports editor of his high school newspaper and his hometown daily newspaper, the Rochester (Indiana) *Sentinel*. Dr. Aylesworth has collaborated on autobiographies with Pete Rose, Alex Karras, and Bruce Jenner, was co-author of *Ivy League Football* and *The Encyclopedia of Baseball Managers,* and is the author of *Science at the Ball Game, The Cubs,* and *World Series Baseball.*

Dr. Aylesworth did his undergraduate and masters work at Indiana University, and took his Ph.D. at The Ohio State University. In addition to his career as an author and editor, he has been a professor of science, writing, and education.

A lot of people had a hand in this book. First of all, not only did Hana Umlauf Lane do a splendid job in pointing me in the right direction and making wise suggestions as she performed her creative job as editor, she also was the one who had the original idea for the whole thing. Then there was John Lane and his beautiful and inventive art work. Finally, I owe a lot to Bea Jackson, who designed it, and Howard Blank, a baseball guru, who kept a sharp eye on the manuscript.

Contents

THE KIDS'
WORLD ALMANAC® OF
BASEBALL

Introduction

Hi! I'm Cal Ripken, Jr. For the past eleven years I have played shortstop for the Baltimore Orioles. Being on a baseball team, at any level, is a great experience. In Little League and in high school I played at neighborhood parks with friends and family. I would often practice with my brother, Bill, who is also on the Orioles, and father, Cal, Sr., who was on the Orioles for many years. Baseball has been, and still is, a lot of fun to play. But along the way I learned a lot about the game and a lot about myself.

There were times when I really struggled with hitting and fielding. Occasionally, I got frustrated. However, I learned that giving up was not the answer. I had to work harder. After practice and games, I would stay and work on my skills. As I began to improve, I realized that hard work and dedication pay off. When my team won,

I was happy, but I also learned how to be a gracious loser and compliment my opponents in defeat.

These lessons have helped me off of the baseball diamond as well. When it comes to education, hard work and setting goals are the best ways to improve your skills in reading, writing, and math. With this in mind, my wife, Kelly, and I established in Baltimore the Cal Ripken, Jr. Learning Center to help people learn to read. These people learn to meet challenges and to use their new skills to succeed in life. Kelly and I also donate time and money to other causes; I was proud to receive baseball's Bart Giamatti Caring Award and the Roberto Clemente Award in recognition of community service. I believe that because I am fortunate enough to play baseball and entertain many people, I have a responsibility to give back to the community.

Included in *The Kids' World Almanac® of Baseball* are many heartwarming stories of players who triumphed over handicaps, and anecdotes on what made the MVP's and Hall of Famers so great. The sections on records, quotations, and trivia are fun to read aloud. I know how much you will enjoy this book. Read it . . . and allow yourself a chance to laugh, cry, dream, and learn.

—**Cal Ripken, Jr.**

Calvin "Cal" E. Ripken, Jr. was born in Havre de Grace, Maryland, on August 24, 1960. He made his major league debut for the Orioles in 1981. One year after earning the American League's Rookie of the Year honors, Cal was named the 1983 American League Most Valuable Player while leading the Baltimore Orioles to the World Series championship. In 1989, he won the Bart Giamatti Caring Award for his contributions to the community of Baltimore for his work with disadvantaged children and adults. Cal had arguably his best season in 1991 when he hit .323 with 34 homeruns and 114 RBIs, while maintaining a .986 fielding percentage en route to his second American League Most Valuable Player Award. In 1991, Cal became the first to win The Sporting News *Major League Player of the Year while playing on a losing club. He also won it in 1983 and is the 20th player to win the Major League Player of the Year more than once. At the end of the 1992 season, his career batting average was .277. He has won two Golden Gloves at shortstop, and has an astonishing consecutive games streak. At the end of the fall 1992 season, he had played in 1,735 consecutive games, placing him second in major league history to Lou Gehrig's 2,130. Cal's achievements have received fan recognition by his being chosen for the American League All-Star starting team ten straight times.*

A Bit of History

The Beginning of Baseball

ABNER DOUBLEDAY
DID NOT INVENT BASEBALL

In spite of all the American folklore on the subject, Abner Doubleday did *not* invent baseball in Cooperstown, New York, in 1839. The National Baseball Hall of Fame and Museum, Inc. is located in that charming little upstate New York town, and the annual Hall of Fame Baseball Game is played at Doubleday Field in Cooperstown, but Doubleday deserves no credit for our national pastime. General Doubleday, a West Pointer who became a Union hero in the Civil War, did live in Cooperstown, but his claim as the inventor of baseball was promoted by a relative. Doubleday neither played baseball nor did he write a single word about it during his long literary career.

EGYPTIANS PLAYED FIRST GAMES
WITH BATS AND BALLS

The first recorded instance of batting contests goes back more than 5,000 years, when Egyptian priests engaged in mock contests with bats. The idea was to promote the fertility of crops and of people. After awhile balls were introduced into the ceremonies. The balls represented springtime fertility and stood for either the sun or the mummified head of the god Osiris. By 2000 B.C., pictures of women playing ball were included in the carvings on the tomb of Beni Hasan.

In the eighth century A.D., these ball games were brought to Europe by the conquering Moors. The ball games were an immediate hit from Austria to France, where they were turned into Christian ceremonies. At the cathedral of Rheims, France, during the Middle Ages, Easter services ended with a game in which opposing teams either kicked a ball or batted it with a stick.

THE BRITISH CALLED IT STOOLBALL.

The English developed the French game into one called stoolball. In this game, the pitcher tried to hit an inverted stool with a ball before the batter could bat the ball away with a stick. Later the game

moved out of the churchyard into the countryside. More stools, or bases, were added, and these had to be circled after the ball was hit. The English children's game of "rounders" was born when a rule was added that a base runner could be put out by being hit by a thrown ball. As early as 1700, posts called "goals" or "bases" were driven into the ground, and the game was named "goal ball" or "base ball." In 1744 a picture book titled *A Pretty Little Pocketbook* was published by John Newbery (for whom the Newbery Medal was named) in London. It contained a rhymed description of the game and a picture captioned "Base-Ball." The book was also published in America several times between 1762 and 1787.

"PLAY AT BASE" IS A HIT IN AMERICA

The new game became popular in America. It was reported that boys "playing at base" in the Wall Street area of Manhattan left their game to join in one of the riots that preceded the American Revolution. And the journal of an American soldier at Valley Forge in 1778 told of the soldiers "playing at base."

In the nineteenth century, baseball in the United States developed from a children's game into a game for adult men. A how-to book called *The Book of Sports* was published in 1834, and it included illustrations and directions on how to play "base ball."

CARTWRIGHT: THE FATHER OF BASEBALL

Alexander J. Cartwright may well be the man who deserves the credit for creating the game of baseball as we know it. He was a surveyor who played with wealthy New Yorkers, and he was selected to head a committee to form a "base ball" club. On September 23, 1845, the Knickerbocker Base Ball Club was organized, and on September 29 the team adopted the 20 rules that Cartwright suggested to standardize the game.

Up to that time, the most popular form of the game had been "town ball" or "the Massachusetts game," and runners were called out when they were hit by a thrown ball. Cartwright's new rules stated that a man could be tagged out or forced out, but not thrown at. He also ruled that there were to be three strikes to a batter, three outs to end a half-inning, and equal distances between bases. An umpire was to be used, and teams were to wear uniforms.

NEW YORK NINE VS. KNICKERBOCKERS

Most historians think that on June 19, 1846, the first game under the Cartwright rules was played between the New York Nine and the Knickerbockers at Elysian Fields in Hoboken, New Jersey. Cartwright was the umpire, and the Knickerbockers were badly beaten by the New York Nine, 23–1. The ball was pitched underhand, and the dimensions of the diamond were still to face important changes. But the game marked the real beginning of organized baseball. Perhaps the first rhubarb in the new age of baseball occurred during the game when J. W. Davis of the Knickerbockers was fined six cents for swearing at umpire Cartwright.

On June 3, 1851, the first game between teams from far-apart cities was played at Red House Grounds in New York between the Knickerbockers and the Washington Base Ball Club. By 1858 there were more than 100 amateur (unpaid) clubs in the northern states. On March 10, 1858, the first baseball league was formed—an amateur league—the National Association of Base Ball Players. The first game charging admission was played between the Brooklyn All-Stars and the New York All-Stars on July 20, 1858. It was held at the Fashion Race Course on Long Island, and 1,500 people paid 50 cents apiece. On June 30, 1860, the Brooklyn Excelsiors began the first baseball tour, starting in Albany, New York.

CIVIL WAR HELPS SPREAD THE NEW GAME

As the Civil War began, enthusiasm in the North for the game seemed to have died down a bit, and many clubs folded. But the war helped spread the game to other parts of the country. On Christmas Day, 1862, 40,000 Union troops watched a baseball game between teams from the 165th New York Volunteer Infantry and Duryea's Zouaves, another Union Army unit. This was probably the largest crowd at any sporting event in the nineteenth century.

The year 1862 was also the year the first stadium designed for baseball was opened. It was the Union Grounds in Brooklyn. But the most significant event of that year was the invention of the curve ball by a 14-year-old boy, William Arthur "Candy" Cum-

mings, of Ware, Massachusetts. He had tossed a clam shell into the ocean and noted its curve. He later duplicated the effect by holding a baseball in a "death grip" and twisting his wrist as he threw an underhand pitch. But he didn't use the curve ball until 1867, when he was pitching for the Brooklyn Excelsiors against Harvard College and curved the Harvard players to death.

BASEBALL TURNS PRO

Professionalism had been sneaking into baseball for several years. As early as 1860, James P. Creighton was paid under the table to play for the Excelsiors. In 1862, players for the New York Mutuals were splitting the money received after expenses from their ten-cent admission at the Union Grounds, and the Brooklyn Atlantics were doing the same at their Capitoline Grounds. In 1864, Al Roach of the Philadelphia Athletics was signed as the first openly professional baseball player.

In 1858, Harry Wright, a cricket professional and jeweler's apprentice, was invited to join the Knickerbockers, largely to help the team defeat their arch-rivals, the Atlantics. In 1869, Wright, who become known as "The Father of Professional Baseball," was asked to head up a professional team in Cincinnati. The Cincinnati Red Stockings became America's first fully professional baseball team. Wright was also professional baseball's first star. He batted .518 and hit 59 home runs in 66 games that year, and was paid $1,400 for the whole season.

After winning their first game against Great Western, the Red Stockings traveled almost 12,000 miles by boat and rail from Massachusetts to California and took on all comers. They played before more than 200,000 people and lost not a game—winning 66 and tying 1. Their tour transformed baseball in the United States by taking the game to the hinterlands and proving that professional teams could succeed.

FIRST PRO LEAGUE FORMED

On March 17, 1871, ten men met at Collier's Cafe on the corner of Broadway and 13th Street in New York to establish the first professional baseball league. Called the National Association of Base-Ball Players, it included the Philadelphia Athletics, the Boston Red Stockings, the Cleveland Forest Citys, the New York Mutuals, the Rockford Forest Citys, the Washington Nationals, the Washington Olympics, and the Fort Wayne Kekiogas. The president was James N. Kerns, who was the representative of the Athletics. The Kekiogas folded in August and were replaced by the Brooklyn Eckfords, who had stayed out of the league because they didn't like the ten-dollar fee required to join.

The league lasted only five years. The Athletics took the first championship, but the next four were won by the Boston club,

which was staffed by Harry Wright and his former Cincinnati stars. The public got bored with Boston's dominance. There was also no way of preventing many players from jumping from team to team. And poor scheduling led to the Red Stockings playing 79 games in 1875 while the new team in Keokuk, Iowa, played only 13. Finally, by 1885, the clubs were riddled with heavy gambling, drunkenness, game-throwing, player desertion, contract jumping, and plain rowdiness.

INVENTION OF GLOVE CHANGES THE GAME

In 1875 came an invention that changed the nature of baseball. In the barehanded days of early baseball, the catcher required the nerves of a test pilot. A team might carry only one or two pitchers, but it took a lot of catchers to finish a game. In a game against Harvard in 1875, catcher William "Gunner" McGunnigle of the Fall River, Massachusetts, team wore a pair of bricklayer's gloves. Soon, heavily-padded gloves for catchers were on the market. An 1890 ad for Spalding Gloves listed four different models priced from two dollars to five dollars. The ad pointed out, "No player subject to sore hands should be without a pair."

THE NATIONAL LEAGUE IS BORN

A Chicago businessman, William Ambrose Hulbert, who also owned the Chicago White Stockings (later the Cubs), was disgusted with the situation in the National Association of Base-Ball Players, and decided to do something about it. At a secret meeting in Louisville, Kentucky, in 1876, he convinced representatives from the St. Louis, Cincinnati, and Louisville clubs that his scheme for a new league was sound. On February 2, 1876, he met with representatives of Boston, Hartford, Philadelphia, and New York in a room at the Grand Central Hotel in New York. It is said that Hulbert locked the door while he read the proposed constitution and player contract he had prepared with the aid of Al Spalding (a star pitcher for Boston who was to become a member of the White Stockings). The Easterners agreed to the formation of a new league, and the National League was born.

The constitution forbade gambling and the sale of alcohol on the grounds, made each team play a full schedule, and required each franchise to represent a city with a population of at least 75,000. Each club paid an entry fee and annual dues of $100, and was required to play 70 games, meeting each opponent ten times, five at home and five away. Admission was set at 50 cents (considered rather high for the time), and the team winning the most games would receive a pennant costing not less than $100.

On April 22, 1876, the first National League game was played in Philadelphia, with Boston winning, 6–5. The final standings in that first year were Chicago, St. Louis, Hartford, Boston, Louisville, New York, Philadelphia, and Cincinnati. Hulbert expelled New York and Philadelphia after the first season for refusing to complete their schedules, and fired four Louisville players for gambling. Teams from 23 cities came and went until 1900, when the National League settled into the eight franchises it would maintain for 53 years.

ALL-OUT WAR AS NEW LEAGUE IS FORMED

In 1882, a new league was formed around the nucleus of the Cincinnati club that had been expelled at the end of the 1880 season from the National League for permitting Sunday games and liquor on the grounds. It was the American Association of Base Ball Clubs. The new league played Sunday games and allowed liquor in the stands. More important, the games only cost 25 cents. It was all-out war, and in 1883, National League president A. G. Mills brought about a National Agreement, a sort of peace treaty. It granted mutual protection on player contracts and even suggested post-season playoffs between league champions.

In 1884, both major leagues faced a challenge from St. Louis millionaire Henry V. Lucas, whose Union Association lured away many players. The National League and the American Association raided so many of the Union's players that the new league was reduced from 12 to five franchises by the end of the year, and it folded after a single season.

1890: A DISASTER YEAR

In 1890 came a more serious threat by the National Brotherhood of Professional Players, an organization that had been formed in 1885. They resented such things as salary ceilings, arbitrary fines, and other abuses by the club owners. Eighty percent of the National League's players, including the entire Washington team, left to join the Brotherhood's newly formed Players' League in 1890.

The 1890 season was a disaster for all three leagues. Over the winter the debt-ridden Players' League, represented by former New York Giant John Montgomery Ward, was out-maneuvered and dissolved by the National League. The crippled American Association barely made it through the 1891 season. Then it folded and the National League acquired its Baltimore, St. Louis, Washington, and Louisville clubs, bringing its roster to 12 teams. With only one league in the business, peace had come back to professional baseball.

From 1894 to 1897 the first- and second-place teams in the National League battled for a gaudy trophy called the Temple Cup. No one seemed too interested in the outcome, and, after Baltimore beat Boston 4 games to 1 in 1897, the whole idea was dropped.

FINALLY, A STRONG RIVAL LEAGUE IS FORMED

In 1899 the American League was formed, an occurence that led to the two major leagues we know today. Ban Johnson and Charles A. Comiskey, both of whom had played baseball in college (Comiskey also played professionally), met in 1892 in Cincinnati, where Johnson was a sportswriter for the *Commercial Gazette* and Comiskey was managing the Reds. They soon found out that they both disliked the National League and the power that the owners wielded.

With Comiskey's help, Johnson became president of the newly reorganized Western League, the strongest of the minors, in 1893. In 1894, Comiskey took over the Western League's franchise in Sioux City, Iowa, and moved it to St. Paul, Minnesota. That same year, Cornelius McGillicuddy, a former major league catcher known simply as Connie Mack, bought the league's Milwaukee franchise, which he eventually moved to Philadelphia.

The league got the financial backing of coal magnate Charles Somers, and in October, 1899, Johnson renamed his league the American League. It was still a minor league operation, but in 1900 the National League cut its roster to eight clubs, and Johnson picked up the Cleveland franchise.

THE AMERICAN LEAGUE GOES MAJOR

Johnson announced that the American League would be a major league in 1901 and withdrew from the minor-league National Agreement. Johnson placed franchises in three National League cities—Chicago, Philadelphia, and Boston—to compete with the American League franchises in Detroit, Cleveland, Baltimore, Washington, and Milwaukee. In 1902, Milwaukee was replaced by St. Louis (because St. Louis was the largest Midwestern city other than Chicago that didn't ban Sunday baseball), and in 1903, Baltimore was replaced by New York.

The order of finish in the American League in 1901 was Chicago, Boston, Detroit, Philadelphia, Baltimore, Washington, Cleveland, and Milwaukee. In 1902, the National League was trying its best to ignore the upstarts, but that year the Americans actually outdrew the Nationals in attendance, by 2,200,000 to 1,682,000. Even more

embarrassing was the fact that the American League teams outdrew the National League teams in the four cities to have teams in both leagues—Boston, Chicago, New York, and St. Louis.

Early in 1903 a National Commission was formed to oversee major league baseball. The commission consisted of Harry C. Pulliam and Ban Johnson, the presidents of the National and American leagues, respectively; commissioner-at-large August Herrmann, the owner of the Cincinnati ball club; and a non-voting secretary. The way was clear for a World Series between the two leagues, the American League was recognized as a major league, and professional baseball entered the modern era.

The Longest, Shortest, and Most Memorable

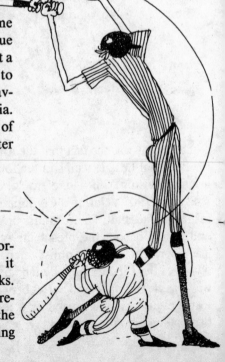

Baseball has always been a game of statistics. It seems that true baseball fans are never without a pencil and a piece of paper to keep score, figure out batting averages, or write down trivia. They keep track of all kinds of records, and when a batter breaks Hank Aaron's top performance of 2,297 career RBIs, it will go into the record books. Here are some of the many records that have been set by the men who have made a living playing a kid's game.

The Oldest and the Youngest

Oldest Rookie Manager: On June 18, 1960, the New York Giants fired manager Billy Rigney and hired Tom Sheehan to pilot the club. Sheehan was born March 31, 1894 in Grand Ridge, Illinois, and had been a right-handed pitcher for six years (1915–1916, 1921, 1924–1926) in the major leagues. At 66 years, two months, and 18 days, he was the oldest man to be named a first-time manager.

Oldest Home Run Hitter: In the first Oldtimer's All-Star Classic, played on July 19, 1982 at Washington's RFK Stadium before 29,000 fans, the American League Oldtimers beat the National League Oldtimers 7–2. Luke Appling, the Hall of Fame shortstop for the Chicago White Sox (1930–1950), hit a home run over the left field fence off pitcher Warren Spahn. Appling was 75 years old.

Oldest Regular Season Hitter: Saturnino Orestes Armas Arrieta "Minnie" Minoso, who had played the outfield for various clubs (1949, 1951–1964, 1976, 1980), got his last major league hit as the designated hitter for the Chicago White Sox on September 12, 1976. The hit was a single and he was 53 years old.

Oldest Shutout Pitcher: On August 6, 1952, Hall of Fame pitcher Leroy Robert "Satchel" Paige, at the age of 47, pitched a complete game shutout for the St. Louis Browns, beating the Detroit Tigers 1-0 in 12 innings.

Oldest Major League Player: On September 25, 1965, the same Satchel Paige, aged 60, took the mound for the Kansas City Athletics and pitched three scoreless innings against the Red Sox. He gave up only one hit—to Carl Yastrzemski.

Oldest Batting Leader: Ted Williams played his whole career in the outfield for the Boston Red Sox (1939-1942, 1946-1960) before being elected to the Hall of Fame. In 1958, at age 40, he won the American League batting title with a .328 average.

Youngest Rookie Manager: Roger Peckinpaugh played shortstop in the major leagues for 17 years. But on September 16, 1914, at the tender age of 23, he was appointed manager of the New York Yankees.

Youngest Player: On June 10, 1944, Joe Nuxhall found himself on the mound for the Cincinnati Reds in a game with the St. Louis Cardinals. He was 15 years, ten months, and 11 days old that day. Nuxhall had been signed by the Reds during World War II when baseball talent was hard to find out of the service. Nuxhall, a left-hander, pitched two-thirds of an inning, gave up six runs, and was part of a 18-0 shellacking by the Cards. He came back from the military and the minors in 1952 and pitched for 15 successful years for the Reds and the Kansas City Athletics.

Youngest Home Run Hitter: Tommy "Buckshot" Brown played shortstop for the Brooklyn Dodgers (1944-1945, 1947-1951), the Philadelphia Phillies (1951-1952), and the Chicago Cubs (1952-1953). On August 20, 1945, at the age of 17 years, eight months, and 14 days, he hit a home run in Ebbets Field in Brooklyn against Preacher Roe of the Pittsburgh Pirates.

Youngest World Series Player: In his first year with the New York Yankees, Hall of Fame third baseman-outfielder Freddie Lindstrom appeared in the World Series at the age of 18 years, ten months, and 13 days. He did amazingly well, batting .333 with ten hits, and went on to a fine 13-year career, retiring to coach the Northwestern University baseball team.

The Longest and the Shortest

Longest Consecutive Game Playing Streak: New York Yankees superstar and Hall of Famer Lou Gehrig played first base for the club for 17 years (1923–1939), and from 1925–1939 he played in 2,130 consecutive games. During that streak he also played in 34 World Series games, making a total of 2,164.

Longest Baseball Throw: On October 12, 1912, Sheldon "Larry" LeJeune, who had played the outfield for the Brooklyn Dodgers the year before, threw a baseball 426 feet 9½ inches. This was well over the distance from the center field wall to home plate in most ball parks.

Longest Career: James "Deacon" McGuire, a catcher, played on 12 teams in 26 years (1884–1888, 1890–1910, 1912), and appeared in 1,781 games. The modern record is held by Jim Kaat, a pitcher who played for six teams (1959–1983) in 25 years.

Longest Home Run: Perhaps the longest major league home run was hit by New York Yankees outfielder Mickey Mantle on April 17, 1953. He cleared the bleachers at Griffith Stadium in Washington with a 565-foot blast off Chuck Stobbs of the Senators in the fifth inning of the Yankees' 7–3 victory. Other stellar homers were hit by Willie Stargell, the Pittsburgh Pirates outfielder (the only player to hit a ball out of Dodger Stadium—506 feet—August 5, 1959); Dick Allen, the Philadelphia Phillies third baseman (529 feet in Connie Mack Stadium—May 29, 1965); and Frank Robinson, the Baltimore Orioles outfielder (the only player to hit a ball out of Baltimore's Memorial Stadium—541 feet—May 8, 1966).

Longest Scoreless Game: On July 16, 1909, pitcher Ed Summers of the Detroit Tigers allowed seven hits and pitched all 18 innings of a 0–0 tie with the Washington Senators, the longest scoreless game in American League history.

Longest Tie Game: On May 1, 1920, the Boston Braves tied the Brooklyn Dodgers 1–1 in the sixth inning. There were 20½ scoreless innings until the game was called.

Longest Game: On May 9, 1984, the Chicago White Sox and the Milwaukee Brewers played eight hours and six minutes before the White Sox won 7–6 in the 25th inning.

Shortest Major League Player: Eddie Gaedel, a three–foot, seven–en–inch, 65–pound midget, appeared at the plate one time for the St. Louis Browns in 1951. He walked.

Shortest National League Game: On September 28, 1919, the New York Giants and the Philadelphia Phillies played a game that lasted only 51 minutes.

Shortest American League Game: On August 21, 1926, Ted Lyons of the Chicago White Sox pitched a no–hitter against the Boston Red Sox in Boston. The score was 6–0, and the game lasted one hour and seven minutes.

Team Efforts

Most Runs Scored in a Season: The Boston Beaneaters (later the Braves) scored 1,221 runs in 133 games in 1894.

Most Runs Scored in a Doubleheader Shutout: The Detroit Tigers scored 26 runs and swept the St. Louis Browns 12–0 and 14–0 on September 22, 1936.

Most Runs Scored in the First Innings: In the National League, the Brooklyn Dodgers scored 15 runs against the Cincinnati Reds in the first inning on May 21, 1951, and went on to win 19–1. In the American League, the Cleveland Indians scored 14 runs in the first inning against the Philadelphia Athletics on June 18, 1950, and went on to win 21–2.

Most Runs Scored in a Doubleheader: On August 14, 1937, the Detroit Tigers scored 36 runs against the St. Louis Browns in the two games of a doubleheader.

Most Runs Scored in One Inning: On September 6, 1883, the Chicago White Stockings (later the Cubs) scored 18 runs in one inning. The modern record is 17, by the Red Sox on June 18, 1953.

Most Runs Scored Before the First Out: On May 3, 1911, the New York Giants scored ten runs against the St. Louis Cardinals before the first man was out.

Most Runs by One Team in One Game: On June 29, 1897, the Chicago Cubs scored 36 runs in one game.

Most Runs Scored by Two Teams on Opening Day: On April 19, 1900, the Philadelphia Phillies beat the Boston Beaneaters (later the Braves) 19–17 in ten innings. Boston had scored nine runs in the ninth inning to tie the score.

Most Home Runs in One Season: The New York Yankees hit 240 home runs in 1961.

Most Home Runs in a Game: The Milwaukee Braves hit eight home runs in the first game of a doubleheader on August 30, 1953. They beat the Pittsburgh Pirates 19–4.

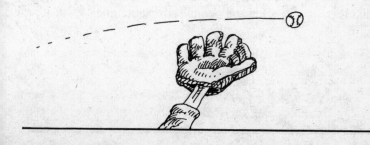

Most Home Runs by Two Teams in a Game: On June 23, 1950, the Detroit Tigers beat the New York Yankees as the two teams combined for 11 home runs. The Yankees had six and the Tigers had five.

Most Home Runs in an Inning: The Philadelphia Phillies hit five homers off the Cincinnati Reds in the eighth inning of a game on June 2, 1949.

Most Long Hits in a Game: On June 8, 1950, the Boston Red Sox had 17 extra-base hits against the St. Louis Browns—nine doubles, one triple, and seven home runs. The Sox won the game 29–4 and also set a record for most total bases with 60.

Most Doubles Hit by Two Teams: The Cleveland Indians and the New York Yankees combined to hit 16 doubles on July 21, 1921. The Indians had nine and the Yankees had seven as Cleveland took the game 17–8.

Most Hits in a Single Game: In the National League, the Philadelphia Phillies had 36 hits on August 17, 1894. In the modern era, the New York Giants collected 31 hits against the Cincinnati Reds as they beat them 25–13 on June 9, 1901.

Most Singles Given Up: On April 28, 1901, Cleveland Indians pitchers gave up 23 singles as the Chicago White Sox beat them 13–1.

Highest Team Batting Average: In the 1894 season, the Philadelphia Phillies had a team batting average of .343.

Fewest Shutouts in a Season: In 1932, the New York Yankees became the only team not to be shut out during a single season.

Earliest Date of Clinching a Pennant: The New York Yankees clinched the American League pennant on September 4, 1941.

Most Batters Used by Two Teams in One Game: On September 11, 1974, the St. Louis Cardinals beat the New York Mets in a 25-inning game that lasted for seven hours and four minutes. A record 202 at bats were recorded. Mets Felix Milan and John Milner had 12 appearances apiece.

Most Pinch Hitters Used in One Game by Two Teams: On May 2, 1956, the New York Giants and the Chicago Cubs each used seven pinch hitters in a 17-inning game for a total of 14.

Most Pinch Hitters Used in One Inning by One Club: The San Francisco Giants sent six pinch hitters to the plate in one inning in a game played on May 5, 1958.

Most Shutouts in a Season: The Chicago Cubs and the Chicago White Sox share the record of 32 shutouts pitched in a single season. The Sox did it in 1906 and the Cubs did it in 1907 and 1909.

The Biggest Shutout Score in a Night Game: On August 3, 1961, the Pittsburgh Pirates beat the St. Louis Cardinals 19–0.

Best Season Winning Record: The 1906 Chicago Cubs won 116 games and lost only 36.

Longest Winning Streak: In 1916, the New York Giants won 26 games in a row—a streak that began on September 7, when they beat the Brooklyn Dodgers 4–1.

Longest Losing Streak: In 1961, the Philadelphia Phillies lost 23 games in a row—a streak that ended when they beat the Milwaukee Braves 7–4 on August 20. The only bright spot in the streak for the Phillies was when they beat the Minnesota Twins in an exhibition game.

Longest Losing Streak at the Beginning of the Season: The 1988 Baltimore Orioles lost the first 21 games of the season, finally beating the Chicago White Sox 9–0 on April 28. This was also the longest American League losing streak at any point of the season.

Most Doubleheaders in Succession: On September 4, 1928, the Boston Braves were forced to play a string of nine straight doubleheaders.

Most Doubleheader Sweeps in a Row: On September 4, 1906, the New York Highlanders (later the Yankees) beat the Boston Red Sox twice, 7–0 and 1–0. Thus they set a record for winning five straight doubleheaders.

Largest Crowd at a Day Doubleheader: On September 12, 1954, 84,587 fans saw the Cleveland Indians play a doubleheader with the New York Yankees in Cleveland.

The Largest Crowd at a Night Game: On August 20, 1948, 78,382 fans saw the Cleveland Indians play the Chicago White Sox in Cleveland.

Smallest Major League Crowd: On the last day of the 1881 season in Troy, New York, only 12 die-hard fans showed up to see their Haymakers play the Chicago White Stockings (later the Cubs).

Largest World Series Crowd: At the fifth game of the 1959 World Series in the Los Angeles Coliseum on October 6, 92,706 fans watched the Chicago White Sox beat the Los Angeles Dodgers 1–0.

Most Strikeouts in a Season: Houston Astros pitchers struck out 1,221 opponents in 1969.

Most Double Plays in a Season: The 1949 Philadelphia Athletics turned in 217 double plays.

Most Double Plays in a World Series: The 1955 World Series winners, the Brooklyn Dodgers, pulled off 12 double plays against the New York Yankees in seven games.

Fewest Errors in a Season: The 1964 Baltimore Orioles committed only 95 errors in 162 games.

Most Errorless Games in a Season: The 1964 New York Yankees played 91 games without commiting an error.

Fewest Errors in a World Series: The 1937 New York Yankees committed no errors in a five-game series. The 1966 Baltimore Orioles went errorless in a four-game series.

Most Errors in a Game: The Detroit Tigers committed 12 errors in a 1901 game against the Chicago White Sox. Chicago did the same in a 1903 game against the Tigers.

Most Errors in a Single Game by Two Teams: The Chicago White Sox and the Detroit Tigers combined for 18 errors in a 1903 game.

Most Walks in a Single Inning: In 1949, an assortment of New York Yankees pitchers gave up 11 walks in a single inning.

Most Men Left on Base by One Team: On September 8, 1905, the Pittsburgh Pirates stranded 18 runners in an 8–3 nine-inning loss to the Cincinnati Reds.

Most Men Left on Base by Two Teams: In 1988, the Cardinals and the Phillies stranded 38 men in a 14-inning game. St. Louis, who won the game 3–2, left 20 men on and Philadelphia left 18.

Heavy Hitters

Longest Consecutive Game Hitting Streak: On May 15, 1941, Joe DiMaggio, who played the outfield for the New York Yankees (1936–1942, 1946–1951), got a hit. He then proceeded to get at least one hit in 56 consecutive games until July 17, when Cleveland Indians pitchers Al Smith and Jim Bagby shut him out. In the National League, Pete Rose, who played several positions for the Cincinnati Reds (1963–1978), the Philadelphia Phillies (1979–1983), the Montreal Expos (1984), and the Reds again (1984–1986), got at least one hit in 44 straight games before going 0 for 4 on August 1, 1978 against Atlanta pitchers Larry McWilliams and Gene Garber as the Braves won 16–4.

Longest Rookie Consecutive Game Hitting Streak: San Diego Padres catcher Benito Santiago had at least one hit in 34 consecutive games in his rookie year—1987.

Highest Lifetime Batting Average: Ty Cobb, outfielder for the Detroit Tigers (1905–1926) and the Philadelphia Athletics (1927–1928), had 4,191 hits in 11,429 at bats for a .367 lifetime batting average.

Highest Single Season Batting Average: In 1894, outfielder Hugh Duffy of the Boston Beaneaters (later the Braves) had 236 hits in 539 at bats for a .438 batting average.

Most Career Hits: Pete Rose had a career hit production of 4,256 in regular season games, plus 80 more in post-season play.

Most Career Singles: Pete Rose had 3,510 singles in his playing career.

Most Hits in a Single Season: In 1920, St. Louis Browns first baseman George Sisler had 257 hits. This included 49 doubles, 18 triples, and 19 home runs.

Most Career Runs Scored: Ty Cobb scored 2,245 runs in his 24-year career.

Most Career Runs Batted In: Hank Aaron, who played the outfield for the Braves in Milwaukee and Atlanta (1954–1974) and the Milwaukee Brewers (1975–1976) batted in 2,297 runs in his 23-year career.

Most Hits in Succession: Two players have had 12 straight successive hits in their careers. Pinky Higgins, third baseman for the Boston Red Sox, did it in four games in 1938. Walt Dropo, the Detroit Tigers first baseman, did it in three games in 1952.

Most Sacrifice Hits in One Game: Brooklyn Dodgers first baseman Jake Daubert had four sacrifice hits in one game on August 15, 1914.

Most Consecutive Pinch Hits: Dave Philley, the Philadelphia Phillies outfielder, hit eight consecutive pinch hits in 1958, and stretched his record to nine by getting another hit in his first time pinch hitting in the 1959 season.

Most Hits in the World Series: New York Yankee catcher Yogi Berra had 71 World Series hits in his career. This included ten doubles and 12 home runs.

Highest World Series Batting Average: Babe Ruth, the star outfielder for the New York Yankees, batted .625 in the 1928 World Series against the St. Louis Cardinals, going ten for 16, with three doubles and three home runs.

Most World Series Stolen Bases: Two players are tied for this record with 14: Eddie Collins, the second baseman for the Philadelphia Athletics (1906–1914), the Chicago White Sox (1915–1926), and the Athletics again (1927–1930), in six series; and Lou Brock, the outfielder for the Chicago Cubs (1961–1964) and the St. Louis Cardinals (1964–1979), in three series.

Most World Series Pinch Hits: The record for most series pinch hits is three, and seven men are tied for this mark:

    Ken Boswell (second base, Mets), 3 for 3
    Bobby Brown (third base, Yankees), 3 for 6
    Bob Cerv (outfield, Yankees), 3 for 3
    Carl Furillo (outfield, Dodgers), 3 for 7
    Gonzalo Marquez (first base, A's), 3 for 5
    Johnny Mize (first base, Yankees), 3 for 8
    Ken O'Dea (catcher, Cubs and Cardinals), 3 for 8

Highest Career Slugging Average: Babe Ruth had a slugging average of .690 in his 22-year career.

Highest Slugging Average in One Season: Babe Ruth had a slugging percentage of .847 in the 1920 season.

Highest World Series Slugging Average: Reggie Jackson, who played the outfield for the Kansas City and Oakland Athletics (1967–1975), the Baltimore Orioles (1976), the New York Yankees (1977–1981), the California Angels (1982–1986), and the Athletics again (1987), had a .755 slugging average in five World Series.

Home-Run Hitters

Most Career Home Runs: Hank Aaron of the Milwaukee/Atlanta Braves and Milwaukee Brewers hit 755 home runs in his career. On April 4, 1974, when he tied Babe Ruth's total of 714 in Riverfront Stadium off the Cincinnati Reds pitcher Jack Billingham, the ball was retrieved by a policeman, Clarence Williams. On April 8, 1974, when he broke Ruth's record off Dodgers pitcher Al Downing in Atlanta, the ball was retrieved by Braves pitcher Tom House from the bullpen.

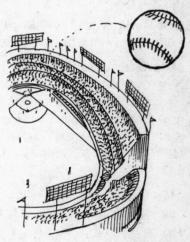

Most Home Runs in a Single Season: Outfielder Roger Maris of the New York Yankees hit 61 home runs in the 1961 season. He hit another homer in the World Series against the Cincinnati Reds that same year.

Most Rookie Home Runs: Mark McGwire, the first baseman for the Oakland A's, hit 49 home runs in 1987—his first full year in the majors.

Most Career Pinch Hit Home Runs: On August 5, 1984, designated hitter Cliff Johnson of the Toronto Blue Jays hit his 19th career pinch hit homer as Toronto beat the Orioles 4–3 at Baltimore's Memorial Stadium.

Most Pinch Hit Home Runs in a Season: Outfielder Johnny Frederick of the Brooklyn Dodgers hit six pinch hit homers in the 1932 season. His sixth homer was hit September 12 in the ninth inning to give Brooklyn a 4–3 triumph over the Chicago Cubs at Ebbets Field.

Most Home Runs in a Season by a Pitcher: On September 5, 1955, right-handed pitcher Don Newcombe of the Brooklyn Dodgers hit his seventh home run of the season as he beat the Philadelphia Phillies 11–4.

Most Home Runs in Consecutive Games: First Baseman Dale Long of the Pittsburgh Pirates hit his record-setting eighth home run in eight straight games on May 28, 1956.

Most Home Runs in Four Consecutive Games: Ralph Kiner, the Pittsburgh Pirates outfielder (1947), and Don Mattingly, the New York Yankees outfielder (1987), are tied with eight round-trippers in four straight games.

Best Home Run Percentage: Babe Ruth of the New York Yankees had a career home run percentage of 8.5, or 8.5 homers per 100 times at bat.

Best World Series Home Run Percentage: Babe Ruth had an 11.6 world series home run percentage.

Most Career Grand Slam Homers: First baseman Lou Gehrig of the New York Yankees hit 23 grand slams in his 17-year career. In the National League, the record is held by Willie McCovey, first baseman for the San Francisco Giants (1959–1973), the San Diego Padres (1974–1976), the Oakland A's (1976), and the Giants again (1977–1980). McCovey hit his 18th grand slam homer on August 1, 1977.

Most Grand Slam Homers in a Single Season: New York Yankees outfielder Don Mattingly hit his record sixth grand slam of the season on September 29, 1987, leading the Yankees to a 6–0 victory over the Boston Red Sox.

Most World Series Home Runs: Mickey Mantle of the New York Yankees hit 18 homers in 12 World Series.

Total, Extra , and Stolen Bases

Most Career Total Bases: Stan Musial, outfielder of the St. Louis Cardinals, had 6,134 total bases in his 22-year career.

Most Total Bases in One Game: First baseman Joe Adcock, who played for the Cincinnati Reds (1950–1952), the Milwaukee Braves (1953–1962), the Cleveland Indians (1963), the Los Angeles Dodgers (1964), and the California Angels (1965–1966), hit for 18 total bases on July 31, 1954. He had four home runs and one double.

Most Career Extra Base Hits: Stan Musial had 1,377 extra base hits in his career.

Most Extra Base Hits in One Season: Babe Ruth had 119 extra base hits in 1921.

Most Career Stolen Bases: Rickey Henderson, who began playing the outfield for the Oakland A's in 1979, had accumulated 1,042 regular-season stolen bases at the end of the 1992 season.

Most World Series Stolen Bases: Lou Brock is tied with Eddie Collins, the second baseman for the Philadelphia Athletics

(1906–1914), the Chicago White Sox (1915–1926), and the Athletics again (1927–1930), for World Series steals. They each had 14, Brock in three series and Collins in six.

Most Stolen Bases by One Team in One Inning: The 1915 Washington Senators and the 1919 Philadelphia Phillies had eight steals in one inning.

Most Stolen Bases in One Game: The record is six, set by Eddie Collins of the Philadelphia Athletics (1912) and Otis Nixon of the Braves (1991).

Most Consecutive Successful Steals: Outfielder Vince Coleman of the St. Louis Cardinals stole 50 straight bases without being caught in 1989–1990.

RBIS, Doubles, and Triples

Most Runs Batted In in One Game: First baseman Jim Bottomley, who played for the St. Louis Cardinals (1922–1932), the Cincinnati Reds (1933–1935), and the Cardinals again (1936–1937), had six hits—including two home runs—in six plate appearances on September 16, 1924. He drove in a record 12 runs as the Cardinals beat the Dodgers 17–3.

Most Runs Batted In in One Season: In 1930, Hack Wilson, the Chicago Cubs outfielder, drove in 190 runs.

Most Consecutive Runs Batted In By One Player: The record is eight, recorded on two straight grand slam home runs and is held by two players. Jim Gentile, the Baltimore Orioles' first baseman, did it on May 9, 1961, and six weeks later, on June 24, 1961, Jim Northrup, the Detroit Tigers outfielder, did the same.

Most Consecutive Doubles: Ernie Lombardi, who caught for the Brooklyn Dodgers (1931), the Cincinnati Reds (1932–1941), the Boston Braves (1942), and the New York Giants (1943–1947), hit four consecutive doubles in four consecutive innings off four consecutive Philadelphia Phillies pitchers on May 8, 1938.

Most Career Doubles: Tris Speaker, who played the outfield for the Boston Red Sox (1907–1915), the Cleveland Indians (1916–1926), the Washington Senators (1927), and the Philadelphia Athletics (1928), hit 793 doubles in his 22-year career.

Most World Series Doubles: New York Yankees catcher Yogi Berra had ten doubles in 14 World Series. He shared the record with Frankie Frisch, who played second base for the New York Giants (1919–1926) and the St. Louis Cardinals. Frisch had ten doubles in eight World Series.

Most Doubles in a Doubleheader: On August 27, 1948, Philadelphia Athletics third baseman Hank Majeski hit six doubles in a doubleheader.

Most World Series Triples: Tris Speaker hit four triples in three World Series.

The Pitchers

Most Games Won: Cy Young, a right-handed pitcher for the Cleveland Spiders (1890–1898), the St. Louis Cardinals (1899–1900), the Boston Red Sox (1901–1908), the Cleveland Naps (later the Indians) (1909–1911), and the Boston Pilgrims (later the Braves, 1911), won 511 games in his 22-year career.

Most Games Lost: Cy Young lost 313 games in his career.

Most Innings Pitched: Cy Young pitched 7,356 innings in his career.

Most Complete Games: Cy Young pitched 751 complete games in his career.

Most Games Pitched: Hoyt Wilhelm, the right-handed pitcher for the New York Giants (1952–1956), the St. Louis Cardinals (1957), the Baltimore Orioles (1958–1962), the Chicago White Sox (1963–1968), the California Angels (1969), the Atlanta Braves (1969–1970), the Chicago Cubs (1970), the Braves again (1971), and the Los Angeles Dodgers (1971–1972), pitched in 1,070 games in his 21-year career.

Most Pitching Appearances in One Season: Wayne Granger, a right-handed pitcher for the Cincinnati Reds, appeared in 90 games in 1969, but was unable to complete any of them.

Most Complete Games in One Season: Right-hander Will White of the Cincinnati Reds started 76 games in 1879 and completed 75 of them.

Most Games Won in One Season: Charles "Old Hoss" Radbourn, a right-hander, won 60 games for the Providence Grays in 1884.

Most Consecutive Games Won: New York Giants left-hander Carl Hubbell won 24 straight games—16 in 1936 followed by eight in 1937. In the American League, the record of 12 was shared by right-hander Walter Johnson of the Washington Senators and right-hander Smokey Joe Wood of the the Boston Red Sox.

Most Consecutive Rookie Games Won: On July 25, 1939, right-hander Atley Donald of the New York Yankees beat the St. Louis Browns 5–1 for his 12th consecutive win in his first full year of play.

Most Career Shutouts: Walter Johnson of the Washington Senators pitched 110 shutouts in his 21-year career.

Most Shutouts in One Season: Right-hander Grover Cleveland Alexander of the Philadelphia Phillies pitched 16 shutouts in 1916.

Most Consecutive Shutout Games: Don Drysdale, a Los Angeles Dodgers right-hander, pitched six straight shutouts in 1968.

Most Consecutive Scoreless Innings: Right-hander Orel Hershiser of the Dodgers pitched 59 straight scoreless innings in 1988, and extended his streak to 67 in the League Championship Series against the Mets.

Most Dependable Pitcher: On August 13, 1906, Chicago Cubs right-hander Jack Taylor was knocked out in the third inning by the Brooklyn Superbas (later the Dodgers), ending a streak of 187 complete games and 15 relief games that Taylor had finished without relief help.

Most Career Strikeouts: At the end of 1992, right-hander Nolan Ryan, who played for the New York Mets (1966, 1968–1971), the California Angels (1972–1979), the Houston Astros (1980–88), and the Texas Rangers (1989–) had struck out 5,668 opposing batters.

Most Strikeouts in One Season: The record is 513 by left-hander Matt Kilroy of the Baltimore Orioles in 1886, but that was at a time when the pitcher's mound was only 50 feet from the plate. The modern record is 383, set by Nolan Ryan in 1973.

Most Strikeouts in a Nine-Inning Game: On April 29, 1986, right-handed pitcher Roger Clemens of the Boston Red Sox struck out 20 Seattle Mariners batters as the Sox won the game 3–1.

Most Strikeouts in an Extra-Inning Game: Right-hander Tom Cheney of the Washington Senators fanned 21 Baltimore Orioles in a 16-inning game on September 12, 1962, which he won 2–1.

Most Rookie Strikeouts in a Single Game: The record is 15, and is shared by two pitchers—Brooklyn Dodgers right-hander Karl Spooner in 1954 and Houston Astros right-hander J. R. Richard in 1971.

st Career Bases on Balls: Nolan Ryan holds the record of 2,755 as of the end of the 1992 season.

Most Bases on Balls in a Shutout: Yankees pitcher Lefty Gomez walked 11 St. Louis Browns batters on August 1, 1941 in a 9–0 victory.

Lowest Earned Run Average in a Season: In 1914, Boston Red Sox left-hander Hubert "Dutch" Leonard registered a 1.01 ERA in 36 games.

Fewest Pitches in a Nine-Inning Game: Right-hander Charles "Red" Barrett of the Boston Braves threw only 58 pitches on August 10, 1944 to beat the Cincinnati Reds 2–0.

Most Home Runs by a Pitcher: Left-hander Warren Spahn of the Milwaukee Braves hit his 31st home run off New York Mets pitcher Craig Anderson on July 26, 1962. Spahn then went on to hand the Mets their 11th straight loss with a 6–1 victory.

Most Home Runs Allowed in a Season: Minnesota Twins right-hander Bert Blyleven allowed his 48th round-tripper of the season on September 29, 1986. Although Blyleven gave up three homers in the game, he won the contest 6–5 over the Cleveland Indians.

Most Career Saves: As of the end of the 1992 season, right-handed relief pitcher Jeff Reardon of the Atlanta Braves, who also pitched for the New York Mets (1979–1981), the Montreal Expos (1981–1986), the Minnesota Twins (1987–1989), and the Boston Red Sox (1990–1992) before he was traded to Atlanta in 1992, had registered 357 saves.

Most Saves in a Season: Bobby Thigpen, the White Sox right-hander, had 57 in 1990.

Most Saves in One Season by a Single Pitching Staff: The Chicago White Sox bullpen registered 68 saves in 1990.

Most Hits Given Up by a Winning Pitcher: On July 10, 1932, the Philadelphia Athletics defeated the Cleveland Indians 18–17 in an 18-inning game. Right-hander Eddie Rommel of the A's pitched the last 17 innings, and, although he gave up 29 hits and 14 runs, won the game.

Most Relief Appearances in a Season: Right-hander Mike Marshall of the Los Angeles Dodgers appeared as a relief pitcher in a record-setting 106 games in 1974.

Most Relief Pitchers Used in One Inning: On July 22, 1967, the Atlanta Braves used five pitchers in one inning against the Cardinals.

Longest Relief Appearance: On June 17, 1915, Chicago Cubs right-hander Zip Zabel was called into a game against the Brooklyn Dodgers with two out in the first inning. He won 4–3 in the 19th after 18⅓ innings of relief.

Best Relief Appearance: On June 23, 1917, right-hander Ernie Shore of the Boston Red Sox relieved lefty Babe Ruth in the first inning of a game against the Washington Senators. No one was out and there was a man on first. The base runner was cut down stealing and Short retired all 26 batters he faced, winning the game 4–0.

Most Career Relief Wins: Right-hander Hoyt Wilhelm, who pitched for the New York Giants (1952–1956), the St. Louis Cardinals (1957), the Cleveland Indians (1957–1958), the Baltimore Orioles (1958–1962), the Chicago White Sox (1963–1968), the California Angels (1969), the Atlanta Braves (1969–1970), the Chicago Cubs (1970), the Braves again (1971), and the Los Angeles Dodgers (1971–1972), won 123 games in relief in his 21-year career.

Most Pitchers Used by One Club in a Nine-Inning Game: The St. Louis Cardinals used nine pitchers against the Chicago Cubs on October 2, 1949.

The Only Double No-Hit Game: Right-hander Fred Toney of the Cincinnati Reds and left-hander Jim "Hippo" Vaughn of the Chicago Cubs each pitched a no-hitter for nine innings against each other on May 2, 1917. Each pitcher issued only two walks in the first nine innings. Then, in the tenth, the Reds scored two runs to win the game.

The Longest No-Hitter: Lefty Harvey Haddix of the Pittsburgh Pirates threw 12 innings of no-hit ball in one game in 1959, but lost the game in the 13th.

Most Consecutive No-Hit Games: Johnny Vander Meer, a left-hander for the Cincinnati Reds, threw two straight no-hitters in 1938. In the first, on June 11, he beat the Boston Braves 3–0; in the second, he triumphed over the Brooklyn Dodgers 6–0.

Most Games Won in a World Series: Left-hander Whitey Ford of the New York Yankees collected 10 wins in 11 World Series.

Most World Series Losses: Whitey Ford lost eight games in 11 World Series.

Most World Series Games Pitched: Whitey Ford appeared in 22 World Series Games.

Most World Series Games Started: Whitey Ford started 22 World Series Games.

Most World Series Innings Pitched: Whitey Ford pitched 146 innings.

Most Innings Pitched in One World Series: Deacon Phillippe, a right-hander for the Pittsburgh Pirates, pitched 44 innings in the eight-game 1903 World Series in which the Boston Red Sox beat the Pirates five games to three.

Most World Series Hits Allowed: Whitey Ford gave up 132 hits in 11 World Series games.

Most Bases on Balls Given Up in the World Series: Whitey Ford walked 34 men in 11 World Series games.

Most World Series Strikeouts: Whitey Ford struck out 94 men in 11 World Series.

Most Strikeouts in a Single World Series: Right-hander Bob Gibson of the St. Louis Cardinals struck out 35 batters in the 1968 series. St. Louis lost the series to the Detroit Tigers, three games to four.

Most Strikeouts in a Single World Series Game: Bob Gibson of the Cardinals struck out 17 Tigers in the first game of the 1968 series.

Most World Series Complete Games: Right-hander Christy Mathewson of the New York Giants pitched 10 complete games in four World Series.

Most World Series Shutouts: Christy Mathewson threw four shutouts in the World Series—1905 (3), 1913 (1).

Most World Series Saves: Right-handed reliever Rollie Fingers saved six games for the Oakland A's in three World Series.

Most World Series Wins in Relief: Rosy Ryan, right-hander for the New York Giants, won three in relief in 1922, 1923, and 1924.

The Only Perfect World Series Game: Yankee right-hander Don Larsen threw a perfect game (no runs, no hits, no walks) against the Dodgers in the fifth game of the 1956 World Series on October 8. He retired the minimum number of 27 Brooklyn Dodgers and won the game 2–0, throwing only 97 pitches.

Best World Series Winning Percentages: Thirteen pitchers are tied with a perfect 1.000 record in World Series play:

Babe Adams (Pittsburgh Pirates, 1909, 1925)—3–0
Jesse Barnes (New York Giants, 1921–1922)—2–0
Jack Coombs (Philadelphia Athletics, 1910–1911;
  Brooklyn Dodgers, 1916)—5–0
Lefty Grove (New York Yankees, 1930–42;
  Washington Senators, 1943)—6–0
Jerry Koosman (New York Mets, 1969, 1973)—3–0
Mickey Lolich (Detroit Tigers, 1968)—3–0
Monte Pearson (New York Yankees, 1936–1939)—4–0
Herb Pennock (Philadelphia Athletics, 1914;
  New York Yankees, 1923, 1926–1927, 1932)—5–0
George Pipgras (New York Yankees, 1927–1928, 1932)—3–0
Ed Reulbach (Chicago Cubs, 1906–1908, 1910)—2–0
Babe Ruth (Boston Red Sox, 1916, 1918)—3–0
Luis Tiant (Boston Red Sox, 1975)—2–0
Tom Zachary (Washington Senators, 1924–1925;
  New York Yankees, 1929)—3–0

Shortest Pitching Career: On July 27, 1918, the Brooklyn Dodgers rookie right-hander Jake Hehl appeared on the mound against the St. Louis Cardinals and gave up four consecutive hits before he was yanked. He never played professional baseball again.

Most Hits Given Up in One Game: In 1936, Philadelphia right-hander Hod Lisenbee surrendered 26 hits in one miserable game.

Most Losses in One Season: In 1883, right-hander John Coleman of the Philadelphia Phillies suffered 48 losses.

Most Walks Given Up in One Game: In 1915, left-hander Bruno Haas of the Philadelphia Athletics, in his only major league game, yielded 16 bases on balls. He also threw three wild pitches.

The Managers

Most Consecutive Games Won by a New Manager: Joe Morgan of the Boston Red Sox won his first 12 games in 1988.

Most Times Fired by the Same Team: Billy Martin was fired five times from his position as manager of the New York Yankees by majority-owner George Steinbrenner.

Best Winning Percentage: Joe McCarthy, who managed the Cubs (1926–1930), the Yankees (1931–1946), and the Red Sox (1948–1950), won 2,126 regular season games while losing 1,335 for a winning percentage of .614.

Best World Series Winning Percentage: Joe McCarthy won 30 World Series games while losing 13 for a .698 percentage.

Most Games Managed: Connie Mack, who skippered the Pittsburgh Pirates (1894–1896) and the Philadelphia Athletics (1901–1950), managed 7,878 games.

Most World Series Managed: Casey Stengel, who managed the Brooklyn Dodgers (1934–1936), the Boston Braves (1938–1943), the New York Yankees (1949–1960), and the New York Mets (1962–1965), managed in 10 World Series—all with the Yankees.

Most World Series Games Managed: Casey Stengel piloted through 63 World Series games.

Most World Series Games Won: Casey Stengel led the Yankees to 37 wins in ten years.

Most World Series Losses: John McGraw, who managed in Baltimore (1899, 1901–1902) and New York (1902–1932), lost 28 games with the New York Giants in nine World Series appearances.

Most League Championship Series Wins: Sparky Anderson, who managed the Cincinnati Reds (1970–1978) and the Detroit Tigers (1979–), has won 18 LCS games—14 with the Reds and four with the Tigers.

Most League Championship Series Games: Whitey Herzog, who managed the Texas Rangers (1973), the Kansas City Royals (1975–

1979), and the St. Louis Cardinals (1980–90), is tied with Tommy Lasorda, who managed the Los Angeles Dodgers (1976–). Both managed 30 games in the LCS.

Most League Championship Series Losses: Herzog and Lasorda are tied with 14 LCS losses.

Best League Championship Series Percentage: Earl Weaver, who managed the Baltimore Orioles (1968–1982, 1985–1986), won 15 LCS games while losing seven for a .682 record.

Other records

Most Career Bases on Balls: Babe Ruth drew 2,056 walks during his 22-year career.

Most Runs Scored in a Single Season: Outfielder "Sliding Billy" Hamilton of the Philadelphia Phillies scored 196 runs in 131 games in 1894.

Most Career Strikeouts: Outfielder Reggie Jackson had 2,597 strkeouts in his 21-year career.

Most Passed Balls in One Inning: Catcher Ray Kaat of the New York Giants was charged with four passed balls in one inning in 1954.

Most Successive Double Plays Hit Into: Outfielder Goose Goslin of the Detroit Tigers hit into four consecutive double plays in 1934.

Most Games Played Without Hitting into a Double Play: On September 29, 1935, Chicago Cubs outfielder Augie Galan played his 154th game without hitting into a double play.

Longest Catch: Joe Sprinz, a catcher for the Cleveland Indians, caught a baseball dropped from an airship at a height of 800 feet in 1931. The force of catching the ball broke his jaw.

Most Baseballs Held in One Hand: Catcher Johnny Bench of the Cincinnati Reds could hold seven baseballs in his right hand.

Most Valuable Players

In 1931, the Baseball Writers Association began to name a most valuable player in each league. The person named was considered to be the best and most inspirational player in the league. Here are the MVPs, their positions and teams, and the final league standings of their clubs.

NATIONAL LEAGUE

1931—Frankie Frisch, 2B, St. Louis Cardinals (first)

1932—Chuck Klein, RF, Philadelphia Phillies (third)

1933—Carl Hubbell, P, New York Giants (first)

1934—Dizzy Dean, P, St. Louis Cardinals (first)

1935—Gabby Hartnett, C, Chicago Cubs (first)

1936—Carl Hubbell, P, New York Giants (first)

1937—Joe Medwick, LF, St. Louis Cardinals (fourth)

1938—Ernie Lombardi, C, Cincinnati Reds (fourth)

1939—Bucky Walters, P, Cincinnati Reds (first)

1940—**Frank McCormick,** LF, Cincinnati Reds (first)

1941—**Dolf Camilli,** 1B, Brooklyn Dodgers (first)

1942—**Mort Cooper,** P, St. Louis Cardinals (first)

1943—**Stan Musial,** RF, St. Louis Cardinals (first)

1944—**Marty Marion,** SS, St. Louis Cardinals (first)

1945—**Phil Cavarretta,** 1B, Chicago Cubs (first)

1946—**Stan Musial,** 1B, St. Louis Cardinals (first)

1947—**Bob Elliott,** 3B, Boston Braves (third)

1948—**Stan Musial,** LF, St. Louis Cardinals (second)

1949—**Jackie Robinson,** 2B, Brooklyn Dodgers (first)

1950—**Jim Konstanty,** P, Philadelphia Phillies (first)

1951—**Roy Campanella,** C, Brooklyn Dodgers (second)

1952—**Hank Sauer,** LF, Chicago Cubs (fifth)

1953—**Roy Campanella,** C, Brooklyn Dodgers (first)

1954—**Willie Mays,** CF, New York Giants (first)

1955—**Roy Campanella,** C, Brooklyn Dodgers (first)

1956—**Don Newcombe,** P, Brooklyn Dodgers (first)

1957—**Henry Aaron,** RF, Milwaukee Braves (first)

1958—**Ernie Banks,** SS, Chicago Cubs (fifth)

1959—**Ernie Banks,** SS, Chicago Cubs (fifth)

1960—**Dick Groat,** SS, Pittsburgh Pirates (first)

1961—**Frank Robinson,** RF, Cincinnati Reds (first)

1962—**Maury Wills,** SS, Los Angeles Dodgers (second)

1963—**Sandy Koufax,** P, Los Angeles Dodgers (first)

1964—**Ken Boyer,** 3B, St. Louis Cardinals (first)

1965—**Willie Mays,** CF, San Francisco Giants (second)

1966—**Roberto Clemente,** RF, Pittsburgh Pirates (third)

1967—**Orlando Cepeda,** 1B, St. Louis Cardinals (first)

1968—**Bob Gibson,** P, St. Louis Cardinals (first)

1969—**Willie McCovey,** 1B, San Francisco Giants (second)

1970—**Johnny Bench,** C, Cincinnati Reds (first)

1971—**Joe Torre,** 3B, St. Louis Cardinals (second)

1972—**Johnny Bench,** C, Cincinnati Reds (first)

1973—**Pete Rose,** LF, Cincinnati Reds (first)

1974—**Steve Garvey,** 1B, Los Angeles Dodgers (first)

1975—**Joe Morgan,** 2B, Cincinnati Reds (first)

1976—**Joe Morgan,** 2B, Cincinnati Reds (first)

1977—**George Foster,** LF, Cincinnati Reds (second)

1978—**Dave Parker,** RF, Pittsburgh Pirates (second)

1979—**(tie) Willie Stargell,** 1B, Pittsburgh Pirates (first); **Keith Hernandez,** 1B, St. Louis Cardinals (third)

1980—**Mike Schmidt,** 3B, Philadelphia Phillies (first)

1981—**Mike Schmidt,** 3B, Philadelphia Phillies (third)

1982—**Dale Murphy,** CF, Atlanta Braves (first)

1983—**Dale Murphy,** CF, Atlanta Braves (second)

1984—**Ryne Sandberg,** 2B, Chicago Cubs (first)

1985—**Willie McGee,** CF, St. Louis Cardinals (first)

1986—**Mike Schmidt,** 3B, Philadelphia Phillies (second)

1987—**Andre Dawson,** RF, Chicago Cubs (sixth)

1988—**Kirk Gibson,** LF, Los Angeles Dodgers (first)

1989—**Kevin Mitchell,** OF, San Francisco Giants (first)

1990—**Barry Bonds,** LF, Pittsburgh Pirates (first)

1991—**Terry Pendleton,** 3B, Atlanta Braves (first)

1992—**Barry Bonds,** LF, Pittsburgh Pirates (first)

AMERICAN LEAGUE

1931—**Lefty Grove,** P, Philadelphia Athletics (first)

1932—**Jimmie Foxx,** 1B, Philadelphia Athletics (second)

1933—**Jimmie Foxx,** 1B, Philadelphia Athletics (third)

1934—**Mickey Cochrane,** C-Mgr, Detroit Tigers (first)

1935—**Hank Greenberg,** 1B, Detroit Tigers (first)

1936—**Lou Gehrig,** 1B, New York Yankees (first)

1937—**Charlie Gehringer,** C, Detroit Tigers (first)

1938—**Jimmie Foxx,** 1B, Boston Red Sox (second)

1939—**Joe DiMaggio,** CF, New York Yankees (first)

1940—**Hank Greenberg,** LF, Detroit Tigers (first)

1941—**Joe DiMaggio,** CF, New York Yankees (first)

1942—**Joe Gordon,** 2B, New York Yankees (first)

1943—**Spud Chandler,** P, New York Yankees (first)

1944—**Hal Newhouser,** P, Detroit Tigers (second)

1945—**Hal Newhouser,** P, Detroit Tigers (first)

1946—**Ted Williams,** LF, Boston Red Sox (first)

1947—**Joe DiMaggio,** CF, New York Yankees (first)

1948—**Lou Boudreau,** SS-Mgr, Cleveland Indians (first)

1949—**Ted Williams,** LF, Boston Red Sox (second)

1950—**Phil Rizzuto,** SS, New York Yankees (first)

1951—**Yogi Berra,** C, New York Yankees (first)

1952—**Bobby Shantz,** P, Philadelphia Athletics (fourth)

1953—**Al Rosen,** 3B, Cleveland Indians (second)

1954—**Yogi Berra,** C, New York Yankees (second)

1955—Yogi Berra, C, New York Yankees (first)

1956—Mickey Mantle, CF, New York Yankees (first)

1957—Mickey Mantle, CF, New York Yankees (first)

1958—Jackie Jensen, RF, Boston Red Sox (third)

1959—Nellie Fox, 2B, Chicago White Sox (first)

1960—Roger Maris, RF, New York Yankees (first)

1961—Roger Maris, RF, New York Yankees (first)

1962—Mickey Mantle, CF, New York Yankees (first)

1963—Elston Howard, C, New York Yankees (first)

1964—Brooks Robinson, 3B, Baltimore Orioles (third)

1965—Zoilo Versalles, SS, Minnesota Twins (first)

1966—Frank Robinson, RF, Baltimore Orioles (first)

1967—Carl Yastrzemski, LF, Boston Red Sox (first)

1968—Denny McLain, P, Detroit Tigers (first)

1969—Harmon Killebrew, 3B, Minnesota Twins (first)

1970—Boog Powell, 1B, Baltimore Orioles (first)

1971—Vida Blue, P, Oakland A's (first)

1972—Dick Allen, 1B, Chicago White Sox (second)

1973—Reggie Jackson, RF, Oakland A's (first)

1974—Jeff Burroughs, RF, Texas Rangers (second)

1975—Fred Lynn, CF, Boston Red Sox (first)

1976—Thurman Munson, C, New York Yankees (first)

1977—Rod Carew, 1B, Minnesota Twins (fourth)

1978—Jim Rice, LF, Boston Red Sox (second)

1979—Don Baylor, LF, California Angels (first)

1980—George Brett, 3B, Kansas City Royals (first)

1981—Rollie Fingers, P, Milwaukee Brewers (first)

1982—Robin Yount, SS, Milwaukee Brewers (first)

1983—Cal Ripken, Jr., SS, Baltimore Orioles (first)

1984—**Willie Hernandez**, P, Detroit Tigers (first)

1985—**Don Mattingly**, 1B, New York Yankees (second)

1986—**Roger Clemens**, P, Boston Red Sox (first)

1987—**George Bell**, LF, Toronto Blue Jays (second)

1988—**José Canseco**, RF, Oakland A's (first)

1989—**Robin Yount**, LCF, Milwaukee Brewers (fourth)

1990—**Rickey Henderson**, LF, Oakland A's (fourth)

1991—**Cal Ripken, Jr.**, SS, Baltimore Orioles (sixth)

1992—**Dennis Eckersley**, P, Oakland A's (first)

Cy Young Award Winners

The Cy Young Award, given annually by the Baseball Writers Association of America, goes to the most successful pitcher or pitchers of the year. From 1956 to 1966, the award went to the single pitcher considered the best in major league baseball. Beginning in 1967, separate awards have been given in each league. Here are the winners, their teams, their won-lost records, and the final standing of their teams.

1956—**Don Newcombe**, Brooklyn Dodgers, 27–7 (first)

1957—**Warren Spahn**, Milwaukee Braves, 21–11 (first)

1958—**Bob Turley**, New York Yankees, 21–7 (first)

1959—**Early Wynn**, Chicago White Sox, 22–10 (first)

1960—**Vernon Law**, Pittsburgh Pirates, 20–9 (first)

1961—**Whitey Ford**, New York Yankees, 25–4 (first)

1962—**Don Drysdale**, Los Angeles Dodgers, 25–9 (second)

1963—Sandy Koufax, Los Angeles Dodgers, 25–5 (first)

1964—Dean Chance, Los Angeles Angels, 20–9 (fifth)
1965—Sandy Koufax, Los Angeles Dodgers, 26–8 (first)
1966—Sandy Koufax, Los Angeles Dodgers, 27–9 (first)

NATIONAL LEAGUE

1967—Mike McCormick, San Francisco Giants, 22–10 (second)
1968—Bob Gibson, St Louis Cardinals, 22–9 (first)
1969—Tom Seaver, New York Mets, 25–7 (first)
1970—Bob Gibson, St. Louis Cardinals, 23–7 (fourth)
1971—Ferguson Jenkins, Chicago Cubs, 24–13 (third)

1972—Steve Carlton, Philadelphia Phillies, 27–10 (sixth)

1973—Tom Seaver, New York Mets, 19–10 (first)
1974—Mike Marshall, Los Angeles Dodgers, 15–12 with 21 saves (first)
1975—Tom Seaver, New York Mets, 22–9 (third)
1976—Randy Jones, San Diego Padres, 22–14 (fifth)
1977—Steve Carlton, Philadelphia Phillies, 23–10 (first)
1978—Gaylord Perry, San Diego Padres, 21–6 (fourth)
1979—Bruce Sutter, Chicago Cubs, 6–6 with 37 saves (fifth)
1980—Steve Carlton, Philadelphia Phillies, 24–9 (first)

1981—**Fernando Valenzuela,** Los Angeles Dodgers, 13–7 (second)

1982—**Steve Carlton,** Philadelphia Phillies, 23–11 (second)

1983—**John Denny,** Philadelphia Phillies, 19–6 (first)

1984—**Rick Sutcliffe,** Chicago Cubs, 16–1 (first)

1985—**Dwight Gooden,** New York Mets, 24–4 (second)

1986—**Mike Scott,** Houston Astros, 18–10 (first)

1987—**Steve Bedrosian,** Philadelphia Phillies, 5–3 with 40 saves (fourth)

1988—**Orel Hershiser,** Los Angeles Dodgers, 23–8 (first)

1989—**Mark Davis,** San Diego Padres, 4-3 with 44 saves (second)

1990—**Doug Drabek,** Pittsburgh Pirates, 15–14 (first)

1991—**Tom Glavine,** Atlanta Braves, 20–21 (first)

1992—**Gregg Maddux,** Chicago Cubs, 20–11 (fourth)

AMERICAN LEAGUE

1967—**Jim Lonborg,** Boston Red Sox, 22–9 (first)

1968—**Denny McLain,** Detroit Tigers, 31–6 (first)

1969—**(tie) Denny McLain,** Detroit Tigers, 24–9 (second); **Mike Cuellar,** Baltimore Orioles, 23–11 (first)

1970—**Jim Perry,** Minnesota Twins, 24–12 (first)

1971—**Vida Blue,** Oakland A's, 24–8 (first)

1972—**Gaylord Perry,** Cleveland Indians, 24–16 (fifth)

1973—**Jim Palmer,** Baltimore Orioles, 22–9 (first)

1974—**Catfish Hunter,** Oakland A's, 25–12 (first)

1975—**Jim Palmer,** Baltimore Orioles, 23–11 (second)

1976—**Jim Palmer,** Baltimore Orioles, 22–13 (second)

1977—**Sparky Lyle,** New York Yankees, 13–5 with 26 saves (first)

1978—**Ron Guidry,** New York Yankees, 25–3 (first)

1979—**Mike Flanagan,** Baltimore Orioles, 23–9 (first)

1980—**Steve Stone,** Baltimore Orioles, 25–7 (second)

1981—**Rollie Fingers,** Milwaukee Brewers, 6–3 with 28 saves (first)

1982—**Pete Vukovich,** Milwaukee Brewers, 18–6 (first)

1983—**LaMarr Hoyt,** Chicago White Sox, 24–10 (first)

1984—**Willie Hernandez,** Detroit Tigers, 9–3 with 32 saves (first)

1985—**Bret Saberhagen,** Kansas City Royals, 20–6 (first)

1986—**Roger Clemens,** Boston Red Sox, 24–4 (first)

1987—**Roger Clemens,** Boston Red Sox, 20–9 (fifth)

1988—**Frank Viola,** Minnesota Twins, 24–7 (second)

1989—**Bret Saberhagen,** Kansas City Royals, 23–6 (second)

1990—**Bob Welch,** Oakland Athletics, 12–13 (first)

1991—**Roger Clemens,** Boston Red Sox, 18–10 (second)

1992—**Dennis Eckersley,** Oakland A's, 7–1 with 51 saves (first)

Rookie of the Year

Since 1947, the Baseball Writers Association of America has given an award to the rookie of the year. For the first two years, only one award was given—for the single best first-year player in the majors. In 1949, the Association began giving the prize to a player in each league. Here are the players, their positions and clubs, and the final standings of their teams.

1947—**Jackie Robinson**, 1B, Brooklyn Dodgers (first)

1948—**Alvin Dark**, SS, Boston Braves (first)

NATIONAL LEAGUE

1949—**Don Newcombe**, P, Brooklyn Dodgers (first)

1950—**Sam Jethroe**, CF, Boston Braves (fourth)

1951—**Willie Mays**, CF, New York Giants (first)

1952—**Joe Black**, P, Brooklyn Dodgers (first)

1953—**Jim Gilliam**, 2B, Brooklyn Dodgers (first)

1958—**Orlando Cepeda**, 1B, San Francisco Giants (third)

1959—**Willie McCovey**, 1B, San Francisco Giants (third)

1960—**Frank Howard**, RF, Los Angeles Dodgers (fourth)

1961—**Billy Williams**, LF, Chicago Cubs (seventh)

1962—**Ken Hubbs**, 2B, Chicago Cubs (ninth)

1963—**Pete Rose**, 2B, Cincinnati Reds (fifth)

1964—**Richie Allen**, 3B, Philadelphia Phillies (third)

1965—**Jim Lefebvre**, 2B, Los Angeles Dodgers (first)

1954—**Wally Moon**, CF, St. Louis Cardinals (sixth)

1955—**Bill Virdon**, CF, St. Louis Cardinals (seventh)

1956—**Frank Robinson**, LF, Cincinnati Reds (third)

1957—**Jack Sanford**, P, Philadelphia Phillies (fifth)

1966—**Tommy Helms**, 3B, Cincinnati Reds (seventh)

1967—**Tom Seaver**, P, New York Mets (tenth)

1968—**Johnny Bench**, C, Cincinnati Reds (fourth)

1969—**Ted Sizemore**, 2B, Los Angeles Dodgers (fourth)

1970—**Carl Morton,** P, Montreal Expos (sixth)

1971—**Earl Williams,** C, Atlanta Braves (third)

1972—**Jon Matlack,** P, New York Mets (third)

1973—**Gary Matthews,** LF, San Francisco Giants (third)

1974—**Bake McBride,** CF, St. Louis Cardinals (second)

1975—**John Montefusco,** P, San Francisco Giants (third)

1976—**(tie) Butch Metzger,** P, San Diego Padres (fifth); **Pat Zachry,** P, Cincinnati Reds (first)

1977—**Andre Dawson,** CF, Montreal Expos (fifth)

1978—**Bob Horner,** 3B, Atlanta Braves (sixth)

1979—**Rick Sutcliffe,** P, Los Angeles Dodgers (third)

1980—**Steve Howe,** P, Los Angeles Dodgers (second)

1981—**Fernando Valenzuela,** P, Los Angeles Dodgers (second)

1982—**Steve Sax,** 2B, Los Angeles Dodgers (second)

1983—**Darryl Strawberry,** RF, New York Mets (sixth)

1984—**Dwight Gooden,** P, New York Mets (second)

1985—**Vince Coleman,** LF, St. Louis Cardinals (first)

1986—**Todd Worrell,** P, St. Louis Cardinals (third)

1987—**Benito Santiago,** C, San Diego Padres (sixth)

1988—**Chris Sabo,** 3B, Cincinnati Reds (second)

1989—**Jerome Walton,** CF, Chicago Cubs (first)

1990—**Dave Justice,** RF, Atlanta Braves (sixth)

1991—**Jeff Bagwell,** 1B, Houston Astros (sixth)

1992—**Eric Karros,** 1B, Los Angeles Dodgers (sixth)

American League

1949—**Roy Sievers,** LF, St. Louis Browns (seventh)

1950—**Walt Dropo,** 1B, Boston Red Sox (third)

1951—**Gil McDougald,** 3B, New York Yankees (first)

1952—**Harry Bird,** P, Philadelphia Athletics (fourth)

1953—**Harvey Kuenn,** SS, Detroit Tigers (sixth)

1954—**Bob Grim,** P, New York Yankees (second)

1959—**Bob Allison,** CF, Washington Senators (eighth)

1960—**Ron Hansen,** SS, Baltimore Orioles (second)

1961—**Don Schwall,** P, Boston Red Sox (sixth)

1962—**Tom Tresh,** SS, New York Yankees (first)

1963—**Gary Peters,** P, Chicago White Sox (second)

1964—**Tony Oliva,** RF, Minnesota Twins (seventh)

1965—**Curt Blefary,** LF, Baltimore Orioles (third)

1966—**Tommie Agee,** CF, Chicago White Sox (fourth)

1967—**Rod Carew,** 2B, Minnesota Twins (third)

1968—**Stan Bahnsen,** P, New York Yankees (fifth)

1969—**Lou Piniella,** LF, Kansas City Royals (fourth)

1955—**Herb Score,** P, Cleveland Indians (second)

1956—**Luis Aparicio,** SS, Chicago White Sox (third)

1957—**Tony Kubek,** SS, New York Yankees (first)

1958—**Albie Pearson,** CF, Washington Senators (eighth)

1970—**Thurman Munson**, C, New York Yankees (second)

1971—**Chris Chambliss**, 1B, Cleveland Indians (sixth)

1972—**Carlton Fisk**, C, Boston Red Sox (second)

1973—**Al Bumbry**, OF, Baltimore Orioles (first)

1974—**Mike Hargrove**, 1B, Texas Rangers, (eighth)

1975—**Fred Lynn**, CF, Boston Red Sox (first)

1976—**Mark Fidrych**, P, Detroit Tigers (fifth)

1977—**Eddie Murray**, DH, Baltimore Orioles (second)

1978—**Lou Whitaker**, 2B, Detroit Tigers (fifth)

1979—(tie) **John Castino**, 3B, Minnesota Twins (fourth); **Alfredo Griffin**, SS, Toronto Blue Jays (seventh)

1980—**Joe Charboneau**, DH, Cleveland Indians (sixth)

1981—**Dave Righetti**, P, New York Yankees (third)

1982—**Cal Ripken, Jr.**, SS, Baltimore Orioles (second)

1983—**Ron Kittle**, LF, Chicago White Sox (first)

1984—**Alvin Davis**, 1B, Seattle Mariners (sixth)

1985—**Ozzie Guillen**, SS, Chicago White Sox (third)

1986—**José Canseco**, LF, Oakland A's (fourth)

1987—**Mark McGwire**, 1B, Oakland A's (third)

1988—**Walt Weiss**, SS, Oakland A's (first)

1989—**Greg Olson**, P, Baltimore Orioles (second)

1990—**Sandy Alomar, Jr.**, C, Cleveland Indians (seventh)

1991—**Chuck Knoblauch**, 2B, Minnesota Twins (first)

1992—**Pat Listach**, SS, Milwaukee Brewers (second)

World Series Most Valuable Player

Since 1955, an award had been given to the most valuable player on the winning team in the World Series. The only time the award has been given to a member of the losing team was in 1960, when the Pirates beat the Yankees in the World Series, four games to three. That year, Yankee Bobby Richardson was selected as World Series MVP. Here are the MVPS and their positions, teams, and leagues.

1955—Johnny Podres, P, Brooklyn Dodgers (NL)

1956—Don Larsen, P, New York Yankees (AL)

1957—Lew Burdette, P, Milwaukee Braves (NL)

1958—Bob Turley, P, New York Yankees (AL)

1959—Larry Sherry, P, Los Angeles Dodgers (NL)

1960—Bobby Richardson, 2B, New York Yankees (AL)

1961—Whitey Ford, P, New York Yankees (AL)

1962—Ralph Terry, P, New York Yankees (AL)

1963—Sandy Koufax, P, Los Angeles Dodgers (NL)

1964—Bob Gibson, P, St. Louis Cardinals (NL)

1965—Sandy Koufax, P, Los Angeles Dodgers (NL)

1966—Frank Robinson, RF, Baltimore Orioles (AL)

1967—**Bob Gibson,** P, St. Louis Cardinals (NL)

1968—**Mickey Lolich,** P, Detroit Tigers (AL)

1969—**Donn Clendenon,** 1B, New York Mets (NL)

1970—**Brooks Robinson,** 3B, Baltimore Orioles (AL)

1971—**Roberto Clemente,** RF, Pittsburgh Pirates (NL)

1972—**Gene Tenace,** C, Oakland A's (AL)

1973—**Reggie Jackson,** RF, Oakland A's (AL)

1974—**Rollie Fingers,** P, Oakland A's (AL)

1975—**Pete Rose,** 3B, Cincinnati Reds (NL)

1976—**Johnny Bench,** C, Cincinnati Reds (NL)

1977—**Reggie Jackson,** RF, New York Yankees (AL)

1978—**Bucky Dent,** SS, New York Yankees (AL)

1979—**Willie Stargell,** 1B, Pittsburgh Pirates (NL)

1980—**Mike Schmidt,** 3B, Philadelphia Phillies (NL)

1981—**(tie) Ron Cey,** 3B, Los Angeles Dodgers (NL); **Steve Yeager,** C, Los Angeles Dodgers (NL); **Pedro Guerrero,** RF, Los Angeles Dodgers (NL)

1982—**Darrell Porter,** C, St. Louis Cardinals (NL)

1983—**Rick Dempsey,** C, Baltimore Orioles (AL)

1984—**Alan Trammell,** SS, Detroit Tigers (AL)

1985—**Bret Saberhagen,** P, Kansas City Royals (AL)

1986—**Ray Knight,** 3B, New York Mets (NL)

1987—**Frank Viola,** P, Minnesota Twins (AL)

1988—**Orel Hershiser,** P, Los Angeles Dodgers (NL)

1989—**Dave Stewart,** P, Oakland A's (AL)

1990—**José Rijo,** P, Cincinnati Reds (NL)

1991—**Jack Morris,** P, Minnesota Twins (AL)

1992—**Pat Borders,** C, Toronto Blue Jays (AL)

The Superstars

What does it take to be a baseball superstar? These men don't have to be handsome, or Yogi Berra couldn't qualify. They don't have to be well-educated, or no one would like Babe Ruth. They don't have to look like Rambo, or nobody would admire Orel Hershiser. They don't even have to be pleasant, or we would never remember Ty Cobb. What they have to be is good, hard-working, and an inspiration to their teams. Here are some of them.

HANK AARON:
Most Career Home Runs
Born: February 5, 1934,
Mobile, AL
Hall of Fame: 1982
Henry Louis "Hank" Aaron
played with intensity throughout his career, even though
his teams were rarely pennant
contenders. Aaron was an
outfielder for the Braves in Milwaukee (1954–1965) and in
Atlanta (1966–1974), and he re-

turned to Milwaukee to become the designated hitter for the
Brewers (1975–1976). His records include the most career home
runs (755) and the most career runs batted in (2,297).

LUIS APARICIO:
Expert Thief
Born: April 29, 1934,
Maracaibo, Venezuela
Hall of Fame: 1984
Luis Ernesto Montiel "Little Looie" Aparicio was a slick-fielding shortstop who was one of the first of many Venezuelan players who were to contribute so much to the national pastime. He played for the White Sox (1956–1962), the Orioles (1963–1967), the White Sox again (1968–1970), and the Red Sox (1971–1973). He led the league in stolen bases for nine straight years (1956–1964).

LUKE APPLING:
Master of the Foul Ball
Born: April 2, 1909,
High Point, NC
Died: January 3, 1991,
Cumming, GA
Hall of Fame: 1964
Lucius Benjamin "Luke" "Old Aches and Pains" Appling seemed to be able to foul off any number of pitches until he

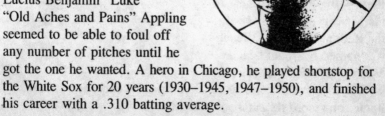

got the one he wanted. A hero in Chicago, he played shortstop for the White Sox for 20 years (1930–1945, 1947–1950), and finished his career with a .310 batting average.

ERNIE BANKS:
Cubs Hero
Born: January 31, 1931,
Dallas, TX
Hall of Fame: 1977
Ernest "Ernie" "Mr. Cub"
Banks was the most enthusiastic
baseball player of his time.
Primarily a first baseman-short-
stop, he played for the Cubs
for 19 years (1953–1971), and
was twice named Most Valu-
able Player in the National
League (1958, 1959)— the first player to be named in two straight
years—although the Cubs finished fifth in both those years.

JOHNNY BENCH:
Golden Glover
Born: December 7, 1947,
Oklahoma City, OK
Hall of Fame: 1989
Johnny Lee Bench, an all-star
playing with all-stars, was the
backbone of the Cincinnati
Reds', "Big Red Machine." In
his 17 years as a catcher with
the Reds (1967–1983), Bench
was named National League
Most Valuable Player (1970,
1972), won 10 Gold Gloves for fielding excellence, and set the
home run record for catchers with 389.

YOGI BERRA:
Star Catcher and Manager
Born: May 12, 1925,
St. Louis, MO
Hall of Fame: 1972
Lawrence Peter "Yogi"
Berra, the ever-cheerful, was as
well-known for his humorous
misuse of words as he was for his
brilliant career as a catcher.
His friend, former player and
sportscaster Joe Garagiola, once
said, "Yogi doesn't say funny
things. He says things funny." Berra

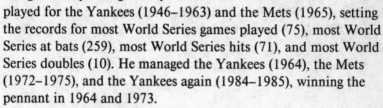

played for the Yankees (1946–1963) and the Mets (1965), setting
the records for most World Series games played (75), most World
Series at bats (259), most World Series hits (71), and most World
Series doubles (10). He managed the Yankees (1964), the Mets
(1972–1975), and the Yankees again (1984–1985), winning the
pennant in 1964 and 1973.

LOU BOUDREAU:
Super Shortstop and Manager
Born: July 17, 1917,
Harvey, IL
Hall of Fame: 1970.
Louis "Lou" Boudreau was a
slick-fielding shortstop, and as a
playing manager he was an
inspiration to his team. He
played for the Indians (1938–
1950) and the Red Sox (1951–
1952). As a manager, he skip-
pered the Indians (1942–1950, winning the World Series in
1948), the Red Sox (1952–1954), the Kansas City Athletics (1955–
1957), and the Cubs (1960).

GEORGE BRETT:
The Man with the Pine Tar
Born: May 15, 1953,
Moundsville, WV
George Howard Brett has always been a great power hitter, and quite capable of displays of righteous indignation, for example, when he was called for putting pine tar too far up his bat. A third baseman, Brett began his major league career with the Royals in 1973. He won the American League Most Valuable Player Award in 1980 and led the league in batting twice (1976, 1980).

LOU BROCK:
The Fleet of Foot
Born: June 18, 1939,
El Dorado, AR
Hall of Fame: 1985
Louis Clark "Lou" Brock could bat, field, and steal. He played the outfield for the Cubs (1961–1964) and the Cardinals (1964–1979). He set the career record for most stolen bases (938, which endured for 12 years), and led the league in steals in eight separate years.

THREE FINGER BROWN:
Pro at Fooling Batters
Born: October 19, 1876,
Nyesville, IN
Died: February 14, 1948,
Terre Haute, IN
Hall of Fame: 1949
Mordecai Peter Centennial
"Three Finger" "Miner" Brown
was the victim of a childhood
accident that left him with only
three fingers on his pitching
hand. But his unusual three-fin-
gered grip proved successful.
He pitched for the Cardinals
(1903), the Cubs (1904–1912), three teams in the Federal
League, and the Cubs again (1916), and had a career earned run
average of 2.06, the second best in baseball history.

ROY CAMPANELLA:
Legendary Catcher
Born: November 19, 1921,
Philadelphia, PA
Hall of Fame: 1969
Roy Campanella, a three-
time MVP winner, was 26 years
old before he played major
league baseball because the
sport was segregated at that
time. He played in the Negro
Leagues until Jackie Robinson broke the color barrier in
1947. Campanella came to the Dodgers in 1948, stayed with
Brooklyn until after the 1957 season, when he suffered an automobile accident that left him a paraplegic.

JOSÉ CANSECO
Base-stealing Star
Born: July 2, 1964,
Havana, Cuba
José Canseco, the outfielder
of the Oakland A's, began his career in 1985. He was voted the
Most Valuable Player in the American League in 1988, after being
the first man ever to hit 40 or more home runs and steal 40 or
more bases, all in one season. In 1992, he was traded to the
Texas Rangers.

ROD CAREW:
The Man with the Golden Bat
Born: October 1, 1945,
Gaton, Panama
Hall of Fame: 1991
Rodney Cline Scott Carew
was one of the best natural hitters ever to play baseball. He
played first base and second
base for the Twins (1967–
1978) and the Angels (1979–
1985), and had a career bat-
ing average of .328—seven

times leading the league in hitting. He won the Most Valuable
Player Award in the American League in 1977.

GARY CARTER:
The Human Backstop
Born: April 8, 1954,
Culver City, CA
Gary Edmund "The Kid"
Carter is one of the few baseball
players to turn a whole franchise around. This catcher played for
the Expos (1974–1984), but when he went to the Mets in 1985, he
immediately became the team leader and helped the Mets win
the World Series in 1986. He later played for the Giants, the
Dodgers, and the Expos. He retired in 1992.

ROGER CLEMENS:
The Man with the Golden
Arm
Born: August 4, 1962,
Dayton, OH
William Roger Clemens is
one of the few pitchers ever truly
to dominate a league in one
year. This right-hander came up
to the Red Sox in 1984, and
in 1986 he led the league in wins
(24), in winning percentage
(.857), and in lowest earned run average (2.48). That year he was
named Most Valuable Player in the American League and was the
winner of the Cy Young Award, which he won again in 1987
and 1991.

ROBERTO CLEMENTE:
Baseball Star and Hero
Born: August 18, 1934,
Carolina, PR
Died: December 31, 1972,
San Juan, PR
Hall of Fame: 1973
Roberto Walker "Bob" Cle-
mente was one of the shining
stars of baseball. He was an
outstanding outfielder for the
Pirates (1955–1972) with a
career batting average of .317.
He led the league in batting in
four separate years, amassing

3,000 hits and winning the National League Most Valuable Player Award in 1966. He died in a plane crash while taking relief sup-
plies to victims of an earthquake in Nicaragua. The election committee of the Hall of Fame waived the five-year waiting
requirement for naming a player to the hall, electing Clemente
early in 1973.

TY COBB:
The Georgia Peach
Born: December 18, 1886,
Narrows, GA
Died: July 17, 1961,
Atlanta, GA
Hall of Fame: 1936.
Tyrus Raymond "Ty" "The
Georgia Peach" Cobb, one of
the best baseball players of all
time, was also one of the most
unpleasant. He was known
for sharpening his spikes to in-
jure opposing players, but he
was also known for his hitting. He had a major league record ca-
reer batting average of .367. He also held the records for runs

scored (2,245). Cobb played the outfield for the Tigers (1905–1926) and the Philadelphia Athletics (1927–1928).

ANDRE DAWSON:
Hope for the Cubs?
Born: July 7, 1954, Miami, FL
Andre Fernando "Hawk" Dawson, the slugger and outfielder *par excellence,* began his career with the Expos in 1976. He joined the Cubs in 1987 and immediately won the National League Most Valuable Player Award, even though the Cubs finished in last place in the National League East.

DIZZY DEAN:
The Country Boy
Born: January 16, 1911, Lucas, AR
Died: July 17, 1974, Reno, NV
Hall of Fame: 1953
Jay Hanna "Dizzy" Dean, the right-handed pitcher, was one of the zaniest of the Gashouse Gang in St. Louis. He pitched for the Cardinals (1930, 1932–1937), the Cubs (1938–1941), and the St. Louis Browns (1947). During his 12-year career he twice led the league in wins and three times in complete games and innings pitched. He was the strikeout leader four times, and he even led the league in saves in 1936 with 11.

JOE DIMAGGIO:
The Yankee Clipper
Born: November 25, 1914,
Martinez, CA
Hall of Fame: 1955
Joseph Paul "Joe" "Joltin'
Joe" "The Yankee Clipper" Di-
Maggio's middle name
should have been "Dignity."
Seldom has there been a play-
er so universally admired. He
played the outfield for the
Yankees (1936–1942, 1946–
1951), ending with a career .325 batting average. DiMaggio's
greatest feat was his string of consecutive games in which he had at
least one hit—a record that may never be broken. In 1941, he hit
safely in 56 straight games.

BOB FELLER:
"Rapid Robert"
Born: November 3, 1918,
Van Meter, IA
Hall of Fame: 1962
Robert William Andrew
"Bob" "Rapid Robert" Feller
was a teenage right-handed
fireball thrower when he started
his career with the Indians in
1936. He stayed with the team
until 1941; then, after service
in World War II, he returned to
pitch for the Indians from 1945 to 1956. Feller led the league in
strikeouts seven times, in wins six times, in innings pitched five
times, and in games started five times.

ROLLIE FINGERS:
Fireman for the A's
Born: August 25, 1946,
Steubenville, OH
Hall of Fame: 1992
Roland Glen "Rollie" Fingers
was a star right-handed relief
pitcher for the A's (1968–1976),
the Padres (1977–1980), and
the Brewers (1981–1985). His
341 career saves record is the
highest in history, and he also

racked up 114 wins. That made him one of only three relief
pitchers who both won at least 100 games in relief and saved
more than 100 games.

WHITEY FORD:
The Yankee Meal Ticket
Born: October 21, 1928,
New York, NY
Hall of Fame: 1974
Edward Charles "Whitey"
"The Chairman of the Board"
Ford was a dependable left-
handed pitcher for the Yankees
(1950, 1953–1967). His .690
winning percentage is the third
best in baseball history, and
he led the league in wins three
times. He also led the league

twice in lowest earned run average, games started, innings
pitched, and shutouts. Ford was in 11 World Series, and set the records for most wins (ten), most losses (eight), most games (22),
most games started (22), most innings pitched (146), most hits giv-
en up (132), most walks (34), and most strikeouts (94).

LOU GEHRIG:
Pride of the Yankees
Born: June 19, 1903,
New York, NY
Died: June 2, 1941,
Riverdale, NY
Hall of Fame: 1939
Henry Louis "Lou" "The
Iron Horse" "Columbia Lou"
Gehrig was a great player and a
gentle man. As a first baseman, he
played for the Yankees (1923–1939),
and batted .340. In his seven World Series

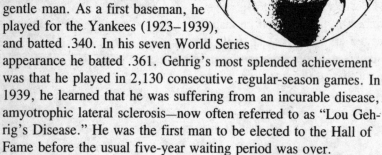

appearance he batted .361. Gehrig's most splended achievement was that he played in 2,130 consecutive regular-season games. In 1939, he learned that he was suffering from an incurable disease, amyotrophic lateral sclerosis—now often referred to as "Lou Gehrig's Disease." He was the first man to be elected to the Hall of Fame before the usual five-year waiting period was over.

KIRK GIBSON:
The Hero of 1988
Born: May 28, 1957,
Pontiac, MI
Kirk Harold Gibson was over
30 years old before he became a
star. This outfielder played for the
Tigers (1979–1987), hit .276 and
was known as a competent player. Then

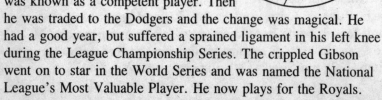

he was traded to the Dodgers and the change was magical. He had a good year, but suffered a sprained ligament in his left knee during the League Championship Series. The crippled Gibson went on to star in the World Series and was named the National League's Most Valuable Player. He now plays for the Royals.

DWIGHT GOODEN:
Mets Phenom
Born: November 16, 1964,
Tampa, FL
Dwight Eugene "Doc" "Dr.
K" Gooden began his righthanded pitching career with the Mets
in 1984, and no young hurler has ever dominated his opponents so
effectively. In his first three seasons he struck out 200 batters or
more—276 in 1984, 268 in 1985, and 200 in 1986. In 1984 he was
named Rookie of the Year, and in 1985 he led the league in wins
(24) and earned run average (1.53). He also won the Cy Young
Award in 1985.

KEITH HERNANDEZ:
Team Leader
Born: October 20, 1953,
San Francisco, CA
Keith Hernandez, the cool, effi-
cient, and brilliant first base-
man, has always been a team
leader. He played for the
Cardinals from 1974 to 1983,
and was traded to the Mets in
1983. Later he played for the
Indians (1990). Always hitting
about .300, he is a ten-time
Gold Glove Award winner.

OREL HERSHISER:
The Comeback Kid
Born: September 16, 1958,
Buffalo, NY
Orel Leonard Quinton "O"
Hershiser began his right-hand-
ed pitching career with the
Dodgers in 1983, going 0–0 and
pitching only eight innings.
But by 1988 he was a star. That
year he went 23–8 and car-
ried a 2.26 earned run average.
He won the Cy Young Award,

was named *Sports Illustrated*'s Sportsman of the Year, and ended the year with a record 59 consecutive scoreless innings.

CATFISH HUNTER:
The Old Reliable
Born: April 18, 1946,
Hertford, NC
Hall of Fame: 1987
James Augustus "Catfish"
Hunter was a steady, talented
right-handed pitcher. He
played for the A's, both in Kan-
sas City (1965–1967) and
Oakland (1968–1974), and for
the Yankees (1975–1979). In his career, he won 224 regular-sea-
son games and lost 166. He twice led the league in wins. In his six
World Series, Hunter won five games and lost three.

REGGIE JACKSON:
Mr. October
Born: May 18, 1946,
Wyncote, PA

Reginald Martinez "Reggie"
Jackson was the consummate
player, and the world knew it.
This outfielder played for the
A's in Kansas City (1967) and
Oakland (1968–1975), the Orioles (1976), the Yankees
(1977–1981), the Angels (1982–
1986), and the A's again
(1987). He led the league four times in home runs, but he set the
record for most strikeouts (2,597). In 1973 he was voted the Most
Valuable Player in the American League.

FERGUSON JENKINS:
The Cubs Reliable
Born: December 13, 1943,
Chatham, Ontario, Canada
Hall of Fame: 1991

Ferguson Arthur "Fergie" Jenkins
was a right-handed pitcher for
the Phillies (1965–1966), the
Cubs (1966–1973), the Rangers
(1974–1975), the Red Sox (1976–
1977), the Rangers again (1978–
1981), and the Cubs again (1982–
1983). He was the pitcher with
the most wins in 1971 and 1974.
Along the way, he won the Cy Young Award in 1971.

AL KALINE:
Tiger Great
Born: December 19, 1934,
Baltimore, MD
Hall of Fame: 1980
Albert William "Al" Kaline
was the most dependable Tigers
player of his time. He played
his entire career in the outfield for the Tigers (1953–1974). Kaline's lifetime batting average was .297, and, of his 3,007 hits, 972 of them were for extra bases.

HARMON KILLEBREW:
Killer Slugger
Born: June 29, 1936,
Payette, ID
Hall of Fame: 1984
Harmon Clayton "Killer"
Killebrew was a legendary power hitter who played first base, third base, and the outfield for the Washington Senators (1954–1960), the Twins (1961–1974), and the Royals (1975). A slugger, he connected for extra-base hits 887 times out of his career 2,086 hits, and his home run percentage of 7.0 ranks third in baseball history. In 1969, he was named the American League's Most Valuable Player.

SANDY KOUFAX:
Southpaw Ace

Born: December 30, 1935,
Brooklyn, NY
Hall of Fame: 1971
Sanford "Sandy" Koufax had
magic in his left arm. He hurled
for the Dodgers in Brooklyn
(1955–1957) and in Los Angeles
(1958–1966). During his 12-
year career, he led the league in
wins three times, in earned
run average five times, in shut-
outs three times, and in strikeouts four times. In his four World
Series, he registered an incredible 0.95 ERA, pitched two shutouts
in eight games, and struck out 61 in 57 innings. He won the Cy
Young Award three times (1963, 1965, 1966) and in 1963 was the
National League's Most Valuable Player.

CONNIE MACK:
Legendary Manager

Born: February 22, 1862,
Brookfield, MA
Died: February 8, 1956
Germantown, PA
Hall of Fame: 1937
Cornelius Alexander "The
Tall Tactician" McGillicuddy,
better known as Connie
Mack, set a record that will certainly never be broken—he
was a baseball manager for 53
years. As a player, he caught
for the Washington Senators in
the National League (1886–1889), Buffalo in the Players' League
(1890), and for the Pirates (1891–1896). Mack was the manager of
the Pirates (1894-1896) and the Philadelphia Athletics (1901–
1950). He won more games than any manager (3,776) and also lost
more (4,025). He won nine pennants and five World Series.

MICKEY MANTLE:
Oklahoma Boy Makes Good

Born: October 20, 1931,
Spavinaw, OK
Hall of Fame: 1974
Mickey Charles "The Commerce Comet" Mantle was "Mr. Reliable" during the 1950s and 1960s—he could always be counted on to come up with the big play or the big hit. As an outfielder, he played for the Yankees (1951–1968) and carried a lifetime batting average of .298, hitting 536 home runs in those 18 years. He led the league in runs scored six times. In 12 World Series, he set the record for most home runs (18), most runs scored (42), and runs batted in (40), as well as for bases on balls (43).

JUAN MARICHAL:
The Pitchin' Magician

Born: October 4, 1937,
Laguna Verde,
    Dominican Rep.
Hall of Fame: 1983
Juan Antonio Sanchez "Manito" "The Dominican Dandy" Marichal was one of the most feared right-handed pitchers of all time. He threw for the Giants (1960–1973), the Red Sox (1974), and the Dodgers (1975). In his 16 years, he twice led the league in wins and in shutouts, all with the Giants. Marichal's lifetime won-lost record was 243–142.

ROGER MARIS:
Home Run Hammerer
Born: September 10, 1934,
Hibbing, MN
Died: December 14, 1985,
San Jose, CA
Roger Eugene Maris was a
quiet man who let his bat speak
for him. It was he who broke
Babe Ruth's single-season
home-run record by hitting
61 in 1961. Maris played the
outfield for the Indians
(1957–1958), the Kan-
sas City A's (1958–1959), the Yankees (1960–1966), and the Cardinals (1967–1968). In those 12 years, he hit 275 regular-season
home runs.

BILLY MARTIN:
The Brat
Born: May 16, 1928,
Berkeley, CA
Died: Dec. 25, 1989,
Johnson City, NY
Alfred Manuel Pesano, better
known as Billy Martin, was al-
ways a fighter—both on and
off the field. As a slick-fielding
second baseman, he played for
the Yankees (1950–1957), the
Kansas City A's (1957), the
Tigers (1958), the Indians
(1959), the Reds (1960), the
Milwaukee Braves (1961), and

the Twins (1962). He turned to managing, and led the Twins
(1969), the Tigers (1971–1973), the Rangers (1974–1975), the
Yankees (1975–1979), the A's (1980–1982), and the Yankees
again (1983, 1985, 1988).

DON MATTINGLY
Yankee Slugger
Born: April 21, 1961,
Evansville, IN
Donald Arthur "Don" Mattingly is one of the purest hitters of the current generation. This first baseman broke in with the Yankees in 1982, and within two years led the league in hitting with a .343 batting average. Mattingly, a Gold Glove fielder, led the league in runs batted in in 1985, the year he won the American League Most Valuable Player Award.

WILLIE MAYS:
A Giant Among Giants
Born: May 6, 1931, Westfield, AL
Hall of Fame: 1979
Willie Howard "Say Hey" Mays was one of the most enthusiastic players of all time—always ready to work his fielding and hitting magic. A swift outfielder, he played for the Giants in New York (1951–1954, 1956–1957) and in San Francisco (1958–1972), as well as for the Mets (1972–1973). Mays was Rookie of the Year in 1951 and National League Most Valuable Player in 1954 and 1965. A lifetime .302 hitter, he had a total of 3,283 hits in his 22-year career, 1,323 of them for extra bases, including 660 home runs.

MARK McGWIRE:
The Young Slugger
Born: October 1, 1963,
Pomona, CA
Mark David McGwire was
one of the youngest sluggers to
make an impression on organized baseball. He came up to
the A's in 1986 as a first baseman, and the very next year led
the league in home runs with
49, winning the American
League Rookie of the Year
Award.

DALE MURPHY:
The Pride of Atlanta
Born: March 12, 1956,
Portland, OR
Dale Bryan Murphy has been
a superstar of the Braves for several years. This outfielder
came up to Atlanta in 1976, and
has twice led the league in
home runs. In 1982 and 1983 he
won back-to-back National League Most Valuable Player
Awards and led the league in runs batted in. He is now with the
Phillies.

EDDIE MURRAY:
Oriole Slugger
Born: February 24, 1956,
Los Angeles, CA
Eddie Clarence Murray hit
the big leagues with a bang. He
came up to the Orioles in
1977 and promptly won the
American League Rookie of the Year Award, batting .283. In
1981, this first baseman led the league in homers (22) and runs batted in (78). He joined the Dodgers in 1989, and now plays for
the Mets.

STAN MUSIAL:
Everybody's Favorite
Born: November 21, 1920,
Donora, PA
Hall of Fame: 1969
Stanley Frank "Stan" "Stan
the Man" Musial is one of the
few baseball players who is
liked by everyone; what's more,
he is universally admired. He
played the outfield for the Cardinals (1941–1944, 1946–
1963), and of his 3,630 career

hits, 1,377 of them were for extra bases. Musial led the league in
hits six times, in doubles eight times, in triples five times, and in
runs scored five times. His lifetime batting average was .331. He
was the National League's Most Valuable Player three times (1943,
1946, 1948).

SATCHEL PAIGE:
The Legend
Born: July 7, 1906,
Mobile, AL
Died: June 8, 1982,
Kansas City, MO
Hall of Fame: 1971
Leroy Robert "Satchel" Paige
was one of the most beloved
baseball players of all time.
He was a legendary pitcher in
the Negro Leagues for years
and, when the color line was
broken in baseball, he was
signed by the Indians. Paige, a
right-hander, threw for the Indians (1948–1949), the St. Louis
Browns (1951–1953), and the Kansas City A's (1965). Paige's best
year was 1952, when, as a relief pitcher, he was credited with ten
saves and led the league in relief wins with eight.

CAL RIPKEN, JR.
Orioles' Iron Man
Born: August 24, 1960,
Havre de Grace, MD
Calvin Edward "Cal" Ripken, Jr.
has been the main man at shortstop
for the Baltimore Orioles since
1981. At present he is about
two years away from breaking
the major league record for
number of consecutive games
played. Along the way, he has
been selected to the All-Star

Game team ten times. Ripken was named Rookie of the Year
in 1980 and won the American League's Most Valuable Player
award in 1983 and 1991.

BROOKS ROBINSON:
Slickest at Third
Born: May 18, 1937,
Little Rock, AR
Hall of Fame: 1983
Brooks Calbert Robinson was
arguably the best third baseman
ever to play the game. He performed for the Orioles from
1955 to 1977, and of his 2,848 hits, 818 of them were for extra
bases. A 16-time Gold Glover, he led the league in runs batted in
with 118 in 1964, the year he was also voted the American
League's Most Valuable Player.

FRANK ROBINSON:
The First Black Manager
Born: August 31, 1935,
Beaumont, TX
Hall of Fame: 1982
Frank Robinson has always
been an inspiration to his teammates. An incredibly skilled ball
player, he was the Rookie of the
Year in 1956. As an outfielder,
he starred for the Reds (1956–
1965), the Orioles (1966–1971),
the Dodgers (1972), the Angels
(1973–1974), and the Indians (1974–1976). A .294 hitter, he accumulated 586 homers in his 21-year career, and won the Most
Valuable Player Award in both the National and American
leagues. Robinson became the first black manager in the major
leagues when he took over the Indians in 1975. He stayed with
them until 1977, and then managed the Giants (1981–1984) and the
Orioles (1988–1989).

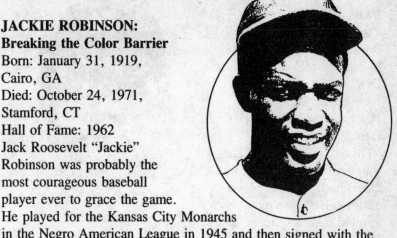

JACKIE ROBINSON:
Breaking the Color Barrier
Born: January 31, 1919,
Cairo, GA
Died: October 24, 1971,
Stamford, CT
Hall of Fame: 1962
Jack Roosevelt "Jackie"
Robinson was probably the
most courageous baseball
player ever to grace the game.
He played for the Kansas City Monarchs
in the Negro American League in 1945 and then signed with the
Dodgers organization. After an internship in the International
League, he became the first black player in modern major league
history. Primarily a second baseman, he starred for the Brooklyn
Dodgers (1947–1956). He was Rookie of the Year in 1947, and
National League Most Valuable Player in 1949, the same year in
which he led the league with a .342 batting average.

PETE ROSE:
The Spirit of Cincinnati
Born: April 14, 1941,
Cincinnati, OH
Peter Edward "Pete" "Charlie
Hustle" Rose was the most dedicated baseball player in the
game. Rose played several positions in the infield and outfield
for the Reds (1963–1978 and
1984–1986), the Phillies
(1979–1983), and the Expos
(1984). Rose was National League Rookie of the Year in 1963,
the Most Valuable Player in the National League in 1973, and
the batting champion of the National League in 1968, 1969, and
1973. Rose was banned from baseball for life for "acts detrimen-
tal" to the game, and served a prison sentence for tax problems.

BABE RUTH:
The Yankee Phenomenon
Born: February 6, 1895,
Baltimore, MD
Died August 16, 1948,
New York, NY.
Hall of Fame: 1936
George Herman "Babe"
"The Sultan of Swat" "The
Bambino" Ruth was the most
charismatic baseball player of
all time. He began his career
as a left-handed pitcher, and

won three World Series games in 1916 and 1917 while losing
none. But he was soon sent to the outfield to take advantage of his
hitting ability. Ruth played for the Red Sox (1914–1919), the
Yankees (1920–1934), and the Boston Braves (1935). He led the
league twelve times in home runs, ending up with 714, plus 15 in
the World Series. He also scored a phenomenal 2,174 runs and batted in 2,211 runs.

NOLAN RYAN:
Strikeout King
Born: January 31, 1947,
Refugio, TX
Lynn Nolan Ryan is the most
awesome strikeout pitcher in
history. This right-hander has
hurled for the Mets (1966–
1971), the Angels (1972–
1979), the Astros (1980–1988),
and the Rangers (1989–), and
in 1982 had the lowest earned
run average in the National
League. He has led the league
in strikeouts eight times and has
seven no-hitters to his credit.

BRET SABERHAGEN:
Stopper of the Royals
Born: April 11, 1964,
Chicago Heights, IL
Bret William Saberhagen is
the star right-handed pitcher for
the Royals. He broke into the
game in 1984, and in 1985, he
won the Cy Young Award in the American league by going 20–6.
He was named the World Series Most Valuable Player when he
went 2–0 in the 1985 Fall Classic. He joined the Mets in 1992.

RYNE SANDBERG:
Sparkling Cub
Born: September 18, 1959,
Spokane, WA
Ryne Dee Sandberg has been
a key factor in the renaissance of
the Cubs. A second baseman,
he began his career with
the Phillies (1981), and was then traded to the Cubs. A fine hitter
and team leader, he was named the Most Valuable Player in the
National League in 1984.

TOM SEAVER:
The Franchise of the Mets
Born: November 17, 1944,
Fresno, CA
Hall of Fame: 1992
George Thomas "Tom Terrific"
Seaver was a right-handed pitcher
for the Mets (1967–1977), the
Reds (1977–1982), the Mets again
(1983), the White Sox (1984–
1986), and the Red Sox (1986).
During his career he won 311
games, struck out 3,640 batters,

threw 61 shutouts, and won the Cy Young Award three times—in
1969, 1973, and 1975. When he was elected to the Hall of Fame
in his first year of eligibility, it was with the highest voting percentage ever achieved—98.84 percent.

MIKE SCHMIDT:
Pride of the Phillies
Born: September 27, 1949,
Dayton, OH
Michael Jack "Mike"
Schmidt was long the star of the
Philadelphia club. This third
baseman joined the Phillies in
1972, and won back-to-back
National League Most Valuable
Player Awards in 1980 and
1981. He was also voted the
Most Valuable Player
in the 1980 World Series, was the home run league leader in
1974, 1975, 1976, 1980, 1981, 1983, 1984, and 1986, and was the
runs batted in leader in 1980, 1981, 1984, and 1986.

WARREN SPAHN:
The Heart of the Braves

Born: April 23, 1921,
Buffalo, NY
Hall of Fame: 1973
Warren Edward Spahn was
the premier left-handed pitcher
for the Braves, both in Boston
(1942, 1946–1952) and in Milwaukee (1953–1964). He also
pitched for the Mets (1965) and
the Giants (1965). In his 21-
year career, he won 363 games
while losing 245, and pitched 63
shutouts. He led the league in wins eight times and in complete
games nine times. Spahn also won the Cy Young Award in 1957.

CASEY STENGEL:
Comedian and Baseball Genius

Born: July 30, 1890,
Kansas City, MO
Died: September 29, 1975,
Glendale, CA
Hall of Fame: 1966
Charles Dillon "Casey" "The
Old Professor" Stengel began as
a joker and ended as one of the
finest baseball minds in history.
He played the outfield for the
Brooklyn Dodgers (1912–1917),
the Pirates (1918–1919), the Phillies
(1920–1921), the Giants (1921–1923), and the Boston Braves
(1924–1925), batting .284. But he made his mark as a manager.
Stengel managed the Brooklyn Dodgers (1934–1936), the Boston
Braves (1938–1943), the Yankees (1949–1960), and the Mets
(1962–1965). His greatest success came with the Yankees, where
he won ten pennants and seven World Series in 12 years. Stengel's
uniform number was retired by both the Yankees and the Mets.

TED WILLIAMS:
Boston Hero

Born: August 30, 1918,
San Diego, CA
Hall of Fame: 1966
Theodore Samuel "Ted"
"The Splendid Splinter" "The
Thumper" Williams was ar-
guably the best natural hitter of
all time. He played the outfield for the Red Sox (1939–
1942, 1946–1960) and had a
lifetime .344 batting average.
Williams led the league twice
in doubles and four times in
home runs. He led the league six

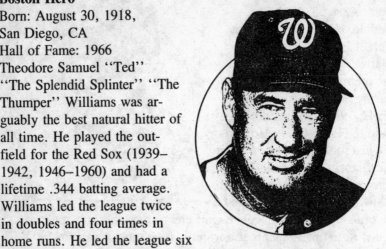

times in runs scored and four times in runs batted in. He was
also a six-time batting champion. Williams was voted the American League Most Valuable Player in 1946 and 1949. He managed
the Washington Senators (1969–1971) and went with them when
they became the Texas Rangers, managing them in 1972.

DAVE WINFIELD:
The Twins Contortionist

Born: October 3, 1951,
St. Paul, MN
David Mark "Dave" Win-
field is probably today's most
talented outfielder, making
catches that most outfielders
could never dream of mak-
ing. He broke into the game with
the Padres (1973–1980) and
was traded to the Yankees to begin the 1981 season. In 1979,
he led the National League in
runs batted in with 118, and
was a Golden Glover in 1987.
He now plays for the Twins.

CARL YASTRZEMSKI:
Boston's All-Star

Born: August 22, 1939,
Southampton, NY
Hall of Fame: 1989

Carl Michael "Yaz" Yastr-
zemski was the pride of Boston
for many years. An outfielder, he played for the Red Sox
from 1961 to 1983. During
his 23-year career, he played in
3,308 games, which was
enough to place him second in
baseball history. A .285 hit-
·ter, he had 3,419 hits—seventh
place in history for the greatest number of career hits—452 of
which were home runs. Yastrzemski, the first alumnus of Little
League Baseball to make the Hall of Fame, won the triple crown
in 1967, leading the league in batting average (.326), home runs
(44), and runs batted in (112).

CY YOUNG:
The Cyclone

Born: March 29, 1867,
Gilmore, OH
Died: November 4, 1955,
Newcomerstown, OH
Hall of Fame: 1937

Denton True "Cy" Young
was such a great pitcher that he
had an award named after
him. A right-hander, his nickname came from the word
"cyclone." He threw for the

Cleveland Spiders of the National League (1890–1898), the Cardinals (1899), the Red Sox (1901–1908), the Cleveland Naps (later the Indians, 1909–1911), and the Boston Pilgrims (later the Braves, 1911). Young won 511 games in his career to place him first in baseball history. He also set the records for complete games (751) and innings pitched (7,356). He led the league four times in wins and six times in shutouts.

Today's Superstars Share the Secrets of Success

MIKE GREENWELL, Boston Red Sox

"You will be faced with some tough decisions as you are growing up that can make big differences in your life and your aim to be successful. You should always discuss these important situations with your parents or even somebody you know who has become successful in areas you are interested in. By seeking good advice you will have a better chance of dealing with tough decisions. The road to success is not an easy one. You will need good habits, hard work, and dedication, as well as sound advice."

WALLY JOYNER, Kansas City Royals

"Always remember that baseball is a team game, regardless of how you are doing individually. While you should always strive to improve yourself as your career progresses, it's also important to do the little things that make your team better as well. Individual stats aren't nearly as important as the overall results of your team."

OZZIE SMITH, St. Louis Cardinals

"You have never failed until you stop trying. I never hit over .258 my first seven years in the big leagues, but I always thought that I could be a good hitter and continued to work toward that goal."

DARRYL STRAWBERRY, Los Angeles Dodgers

"Never give up on your goal. Understand that if you want to become a pro baseball player or a pro in any sport, you have to make sacrifices along the way. I did, and anybody who reaches the majors has to give up certain things in life."

RYNE SANDBERG, Chicago Cubs

"Try to learn as much as you can from your parents and coaches. Practice to improve yourself. Play and have fun."

DANNY TARTABULL, New York Yankees

"Schoolwork is the most important thing. Only a small percentage can make it to the big leagues. That's why you should study hard, because you can always use your education. Remember that baseball is just a game and games are meant to be enjoyed. The people I admire most are doctors, policemen, and firemen. Whatever you decide to do with your life always try your hardest and you will be a success."

DON MATTINGLY, New York Yankees

"There are many similarities in how you should play baseball and how you should conduct yourself in life. In baseball you should always put forth your best effort and that lesson applies to life also. Baseball teaches us teamwork and how to work together for a common goal. Those are the same characteristics that are important in life. Always be respectful of your coaches and your teachers. They are there to help you become better players and better people."

BOBBY BONILLA, New York Mets

"Never lose sight of your goals. I made it. I was a young kid from the Bronx, but I knew what I wanted to do since I was six. Keep fighting and never give up. As long as you work hard, nothing is impossible.'

GEORGE BRETT, Kansas City Royals

"Something that is very important for youngsters to remember is that they should enjoy the game and have fun playing. Do as well as you can, but have fun!"

MARK GRACE, Chicago Cubs

"Listen to your coaches. Always work hard and stay away from vices like drugs and other bad influences."

DARREN DAULTON, Philadelphia Phillies

"I believe education is the most important part of growing up. If you discipline yourself in your study habits, you will be able to apply those habits and knowledge to whatever sport you choose. Consistency is the name of the game in professional sports. If you start early in your life at being consistent at whatever you're doing, things will become easier to achieve later on. Always remember, the more you practice, the better you will be."

DWIGHT GOODEN, New York Mets

"No matter how much success you don't take anything for granted. Nothing is forever. You have to keep practicing and practicing no matter how old you are. All the great athletes, no matter what sport, never lose their work ethics. I have had some success, but I also have had some setbacks because of arm problems. I really have a deep appreciation for what it takes to stay in the game."

CHARLES NAGY, Cleveland Indians

"Being the best you can, be it whether in baseball or any other profession, takes dedication and commitment beyond anything else. If baseball is your choice always remember that this doesn't mean your education can be pushed aside, it is the most important thing you can get and something that nobody can take away from you."

Champions of the World

The World Series between The National and American League Champions has been played since 1903. With the exception of 1904, the Fall Classic, as it has come to be known, has been played annually. Here are facts on the World Series from 1903 on.

1903

Boston (AL) 5, Pittsburgh (NL) 3. The first World Series was a casual thing. It was decided in August that the games would be played, when it looked as though Boston and Pittsburgh were going to win their pennants. Then the presidents of the two clubs personally made plans to have a playoff. At the end of the season, the Boston Somersets (later the Red Sox) finished 14½ games ahead of the Philadelphia Athletics, and the Pirates won by 6½ games over the New York Giants. Boston surprised Pittsburgh in the best five-out-of-nine-game series.

1904

No series. The New York Giants owner, John T. Brush, and his manager, John McGraw, resented the new American League, which they thought was no more than a minor league. So the Somersets and the Giants did not meet that year.

1905

New York (NL) 4, Philadelphia (AL) 1. Brush changed his mind in 1905, and his Giants met the Philadelphia Athletics in the series. The chief interest of this best four-out-of-seven-game series was that it was a pitchers' battle all the way, and every game was a shutout.

1906

Chicago (AL) 4, Chicago (NL) 2. This year was an upset year, and the first time that teams from the same city met for the championship. The Chicago White Sox were called the "Hitless Wonders," because they had a team batting average of .228—the lowest in the American League—while the Chicago Cubs had won the pennant by 20 games over the Giants. Still, the Sox took the series.

1907

Chicago (NL) 4, Detroit (AL) 0, 1 tie.

1908

Chicago (NL) 4, Detroit (AL) 1. The Cubs had a bit of a problem when they ended the season in a tie with the New York Giants. This caused the first major league playoff game to decide a pennant, which the Cubs won, 4-2. Once again the Cubs took the series. The people of Detroit seemed to sense the impending devastation. The last game was played in Detroit, and only 6,201 people showed up at Bennett Field—a record low for a World Series crowd.

1909

Pittsburgh (NL) 4, Detroit (AL) 3. For the first time in history, the World Series went the full seven games.

1910

Philadelphia (AL) 4, Chicago (NL) 1.

1911

Philadelphia (AL) 4, New York (NL) 2. This was a long series—it lasted 13 days because rain forced postponement for six days between the third and fourth games.

1912

Boston (AL) 4, New York (NL) 3, 1 tie. The Red Sox set an American League record by winning 105 games and finishing 14 games ahead of the Senators. The Giants also ran away from the rest of their league, finishing ten games ahead of the Pirates. The series, not surprisingly, given the season records, was a cliffhanger.

1913

Philadelphia (AL) 4, New York (NL) 1.

1914

Boston (NL) 4, Philadelphia (AL) 0. This was the year of the Boston "Miracle Braves." On July 19, the team was in last place. But, after an incredible winning streak, they were in second place on August 10, moved into first on September 2, slipped a bit to third, and returned to first on September 8. Winning 60 of their last 76 games, they took the pennant by 10½ games over the Giants. The miracle continued into the Fall Classic as the Philadelphia Athletics became the first team in baseball history to be beaten in four straight games.

1915

Boston (AL) 4, Philadelphia (NL) 1. This was the year that another Philadelphia team made it to the World Series—the Phillies—with their .592 won-lost percentage, the lowest to capture the flag up to that time. A guest at the World Series was President Woodrow Wilson, who traveled all the way from Washington to Philadelphia to throw out the first ball of the second game.

1916

Boston (AL) 4, Brooklyn (NL) 1. In the second game, Babe Ruth made his first World Series start as a Red Sox pitcher and won the game 2–1. So far, this is the longest game played in World Series history. It went 14 innings, and the Babe gave up only six hits.

1917

Chicago (AL) 4, New York (NL) 2.

1918

Boston (AL) 4, Chicago (NL) 2. The United States was at war in 1918, and the major leagues were ordered to suspend the season by Labor Day. Only the last two championship clubs were allowed to extend their seasons in order to play the World Series. In this series, Babe Ruth, pitching for the Red Sox, ran up his string of consecutive scoreless innings to a whopping 29⅔ innings—a record that was not broken until 1961.

1919

Cincinnati (NL) 5, Chicago (AL) 3. The White Sox finished three games ahead of the Indians this year. They were one of the greatest teams of all time, with stars at every position. In the National League, it was the underdog Reds, who beat out the Giants by ten games. But the Reds won their first world championship. It was a tainted championship, however, since this was the year of the infamous "Black Sox Scandal," in which it was learned that several players on the Chicago team had thrown the World Series. (See page 188 for more information on the Black Sox Scandal.)

1920

Cleveland (AL) 5, Brooklyn (NL) 2.

1921

New York (NL) 5, New York (AL) 3. This year, the World Series was the first "Subway Series." The Giants won the pennant by four games over the Pirates, and the Yankees beat out the Indians by 4½ games.

1922

New York (NL) 4, New York (AL) 0, 1 tie. After a three-year trial of the best of nine games, baseball went back to a World Series of a maximum seven games. The highlight of the series was the second game, which ended in a 3–3 tie. The game was called at the end of the tenth inning by the home plate umpire on account of darkness. Since there was still about a half-hour of light remaining, many of the fans were understandably upset. Thinking that Baseball Commissioner Kenesaw Mountain Landis was responsible for the decision, some fans followed him with a chorus of boos as he made his way across the field after the game. As a result of the disorder that followed, Landis ordered the receipts of the game to be turned over to New York charities.

1923

New York (AL) 4, New York (NL) 2. It was the Yankees and the Giants once again in the World Series. Playing in the brand-new Yankee Stadium, the Bronx Bombers finished 16 games over the Tigers. The Giants had ended the season 4½ games ahead of the Reds. This time, outfielder Babe Ruth was not to be denied. He hit .368, with three home runs (two in succession in the second game), a triple, a double, and three singles, walking eight times.

1924

Washington (AL) 4, New York (NL) 3

1925

Pittsburgh (NL) 4, Washington (AL) 3.

1926

St. Louis (NL) 4, New York (AL) 3.

1927

New York (AL) 4, Pittsburgh (NL) 0. Many consider the 1927 Yankees to have been the best baseball team of all time. They didn't surrender first place all year, and with Ruth, Gehrig, *et al* on the Yankee staff, the series was no contest.

1928

New York (AL) 4, St. Louis (NL) 0.

1929

Philadelphia (AL) 4, Chicago (NL) 1.

1930

Philadelphia (AL) 4, St. Louis (NL) 2.

1931

St. Louis (NL) 4, Philadelphia (AL) 3.

1932

New York (AL) 4, Chicago (NL) 0. This was the year of Joe McCarthy's revenge. He had been dismissed as the manager of the Cubs late in the 1930 season. Now he was manager of the Yankees, and he brought them in in first place. Revenge was sweet for McCarthy as the Yankees swept the series.

1933

New York (NL) 4, Washington (AL) 1.

1934

St. Louis (NL) 4, Detroit (AL) 3. The Detroit Tigers took their first pennant in 25 years. In the National League, the Cardinals beat out the Giants on the last day of the season, finishing two games ahead of New York. The first six games of the series were well-played, but the seventh game was a travesty, with the Cardinals winning in Detroit, 11–0, to take the series. During that game, Commissioner Landis was forced to remove Cardinal left fielder Joe "Ducky" Medwick from the action after an incredible display by vegetable-throwing Tiger fans. They were protesting Medwick's previous aggressive slide into Tiger third baseman Marv Owen.

1935

Detroit (AL) 4, Chicago (NL) 2.

1936

New York (AL) 4, New York (NL) 2.

1937

New York (AL) 4, New York (NL) 1. The Yankees took the series, and they turned it into a debacle. Of the Yanks' total of 42 hits, six were doubles, four were triples, and four were home runs.

1938

New York (AL) 4, Chicago (NL) 0. Once again, the Yankees whitewashed the Cubs in the series.

1939

New York (AL) 4, Cincinnati (NL) 0. The Yankees took the World Series—their fourth straight world championship and the fifth time they had won a series by sweeping all four games.

1940

Cincinnati (NL) 4, Detroit (AL) 3.

1941

New York (AL) 4, Brooklyn (NL) 1. It was the Yankees again on top of the heap in 1941, a season highlighted by center fielder Joe Di-Maggio's record-breaking 56-game streak in which he had at least one hit in every contest. The Yankees clinched the pennant on September 4—the earliest date ever—in their 136th game, ending 17 games ahead of the Red Sox. The Dodgers were the winners in the National League after the lead had changed hands between Brooklyn and the Cardinals 27 times during the season, and they finished 2½ games ahead of the Redbirds.

1942

St. Louis (NL) 4, New York (AL) 1.

1943

New York (AL) 4, St. Louis (NL) 1.

1944

St. Louis (NL) 4, St. Louis (AL) 2. The year 1944 gave baseball fans a contest that will probably never be repeated—an all-St. Louis World Series. The perennial doormats, the Browns, finally won the American League pennant by one game over the Tigers. The Cardinals had no trouble, finishing 14½ games ahead of the Pirates. The

Redbirds won the series, and the key to the championship had been the fielding. The Cardinals made no errors in the six games, while the Browns committed ten.

1945
Detroit (AL) 4, Chicago (NL) 3.

1946
St. Louis (NL) 4, Boston (AL) 3. With Ted Williams back from serving in World War II, the Red Sox won their first pennant since 1918, finishing 12 games ahead of the Tigers. In the National League, it was the Cardinals, but they did it the hard way. Finishing the season in a tie with the Dodgers, they played the first pennant-deciding playoff series in major league history, and won the first two games of the best two-out-of-three series.

1947
New York (AL) 4, Brooklyn (NL) 3. This World Series was the first in which a black man participated—the Dodgers first baseman Jackie Robinson.

1948
Cleveland (AL) 4, Boston (NL) 2.

1949
New York (AL) 4, Brooklyn (NL) 1.

1950
New York (AL) 4, Philadelphia (NL) 0.

1951
New York (AL) 4, New York (NL) 2. The Giants made the most historic run toward the pennant since the "Miracle Braves" of 1914. Starting on August 12, and trailing Brooklyn by 13½ games, they won 16 consecutive games and were only 5½ games behind the Dodgers on September 9. Then they won 16 of their last 20 to force a playoff series. The Giants and Dodgers split the first two games. In the final game, with the Dodgers ahead 4-1 in the bottom of the

ninth, the Giants scored one run. With two men on, Giants third baseman Bobby Thomson hit a home run to win the pennant. The Yankees had less trouble, finishing five games in front of the Indians. The Giants heroics gave out in the World Series, as the Yankees took yet another championship.

1952

New York (AL) 4, Brooklyn (NL) 3.

1953

New York (AL) 4, Brooklyn (NL) 2.

1954

New York (NL) 4, Cleveland (AL) 0.

1955

Brooklyn (NL) 4, New York (AL) 3.

1956

New York (AL) 4, Brooklyn (NL) 3. The most spectacular event of the World Series came in the fifth game. Don Larsen, the Yankees pitcher, was perfect that day. Not a single Dodger made it to first base. That was the one and only perfect game in series history.

1957

Milwaukee (NL) 4, New York (AL) 3.

1958

New York (AL) 4, Milwaukee (AL) 3. The Yankees were the first team since 1925 to win the Fall Classic after being down three games.

1959

Los Angeles (NL) 4, Chicago (AL) 2.

1960

Pittsburgh (NL) 4, New York (AL) 3. The teams split the first six games, and the final game was a free-for-all. Pittsburgh scored two runs in the first inning and two in the second. The Yankees scored one run in the fifth and four in the sixth. In the eighth, New York added two more runs and the Pirates added five. The Yankees tied the ball game in the ninth with two more runs. But then came the bottom of the inning. Pirates second baseman Bill Mazeroski stepped up to the plate, took one pitch for a ball, and then hit the homer that made the Pirates the champions of the world. The Yanks had scored 55 runs to the Pirates' 27, but the Bucs triumphed in the series.

1961

New York (AL) 4, Cincinnati (NL) 1. It was in the fourth game of the series that Whitey Ford broke Babe Ruth's record of pitching 29⅔ consecutive scoreless innings in World Series Play. When Ford won the first game of the 1961 series, he had gone 27 innings without giving up a run. In the fourth game, he went five scoreless innings before he injured his ankle. He thereby set a new World Series record of 32 innings without a score.

1962

New York (AL) 4, San Francisco (NL) 3.

1963

Los Angeles (NL) 4, New York (AL) 0.

1964

St. Louis (NL) 4, New York (AL) 3. Probably the strangest thing coming out of this year's series happened to the managers. The day after the series ended, Manager Johnny Keane of the Cardinals resigned, and Yogi Berra, the rookie Yankee manager, was fired, although he had won a pennant in his first year of managing. Four days later, Keene was named as Yankee manager, and in November, Berra went to the Mets as a coach.

1965

Los Angeles (NL) 4, Minnesota (AL) 3.

1966

Baltimore (AL) 4, Los Angeles (NL) 0. This was a humiliating World Series for the Dodgers. They lost four straight. They managed to score only two runs in four games, going 33 innings without scoring. They committed six errors—all of them in the second game—while the Orioles went errorless.

1967

St. Louis (NL) 4, Boston (AL) 3.

1968

Detroit (AL) 4, St. Louis (NL) 3. The pitchers were the stars of this World Series. The Cardinals' Bob Gibson struck out 17 batters in the first game and ended up with two victories, while the Tigers' Mickey Lolich won three.

1969

New York (NL) 4, Baltimore (AL) 1. This series went to the "Miracle Mets," who had never finished higher than ninth place.

1970

Baltimore (AL) 4, Cincinnati (NL) 1.

1971

Pittsburgh (NL) 4, Baltimore (AL) 3.

1972

Oakland (AL) 4, Cincinnati (NL) 3.

1973

Oakland (AL) 4, New York (NL) 3. The Mets pulled a repeat miracle. The "Amazin' Mets" were in last place on August 30, but they managed to win the Eastern Division of the National League by 1½ games over the Cardinals. The Mets took the Reds in the LCS, but lost a close World Series to the A's.

1974

Oakland (AL) 4, Los Angeles (NL) 1.

1975

Cincinnati (NL) 4, Boston (AL) 3.

1976

Cincinnati (NL) 4, New York (AL) 0.

1977

New York (AL) 4, Los Angeles (NL) 2.

1978

New York (AL) 4, Los Angeles (NL) 2. The Yanks lost the first two games, but they fought back and won the next four games and the series, becoming the first team to win the Fall Classic in six games after losing the first two.

1979

Pittsburgh (NL) 4, Baltimore (AL) 3. After the fourth game, the Orioles were ahead, three games to one. But the Pirates roared back to take the next three games and the championship.

1980

Philadelphia (NL) 4, Kansas City (AL) 2. This was the first Phillies triumph in the Fall Classic.

1981

Los Angeles (NL) 4, New York (AL) 2.

1982

St. Louis (NL) 4, Milwaukee (AL) 3.

1983

Baltimore (AL) 4, Philadelphia (NL) 1.

1984

Detroit (AL) 4, San Diego (NL) 1.

1985

Kansas City (AL) 4, St. Louis (NL) 3.

1986

New York (NL) 4, Boston (AL) 3.

1987

Minnesota (AL) 4, St. Louis (NL) 3. The World Series opened in the noisy Metrodome in Minneapolis, and it was to turn out that the noise of the fans in that enclosed stadium may have made the difference. Measured decibel levels indicated it was so noisy that many people could have suffered temporary hearing impairment. The Twins won all four games there, while the Cardinals won the three that were played in St. Louis.

1988

Los Angeles (NL) 4, Oakland (AL) 1.

1989

Oakland (AL) 4, San Francisco (NL) 0. Although this series went only four games, it took the longest time of any series to complete. After the first two games in Oakland, which the A's won on October 14 (5–0) and October 15 (5–1), the series moved to San Francisco on October 17. Just before the game was to start, the Bay Area was hit by a tragic and massive earthquake. Play was not resumed for ten days, and then the A's went on to take the series on October 27 (13–7) and October 28 (9–6).

1990

Cincinnati (NL) 4, Oakland (AL) 0. In one of the most dazzling upsets in World Series history, the Reds swept the A's in four games. The A's had made mincemeat of the other teams in the Western Division, finishing in first place by nine games and then winning the LCS by shutting out the Red Sox 4 games to none. The Reds had had trouble with the Pirates in their LCS. But in the World Series, Cincinnati batted .319, against Oakland's .209. The Reds also outhit the A's, 45 to 28, and outscored them 22–8. In the entire series, the Reds pitchers allowed zero runs after the third inning.

1991

Minnesota (AL) 4, Atlanta (NL) 3. For the first time in history, the World Series was played between two teams who had finished in last place in their divisions the year before. In 1990 the Braves had finished 26 games out of first place, while the Twins trailed by 29 games. The series was close. The Twins won all four games in Minneapolis and the Braves won all three played in Atlanta. It was the first series to have four games decided as a result of the last pitch; the first to have five games decided in a team's last bat; the first to have three extra-inning games; the first to have a seventh and last game go scoreless through nine innings. In addition to all this, the series had five one-run games and a 1–0 seventh game.

1992

Toronto (AL) 4, Atlanta (NL) 2. The Braves repeated in the National League, but for the first time in history a foreign team (from Canada) played in the World Series. Not only that, but the Canadians went on to win the Fall Classic. It was a close series, with four of the six games being decided by one run. Along the way, the bullpen of the Blue Jays went 15½ straight innings without allowing a run.

The All-Star Game

The All-Star game was first played between the greats of the American League and the outstanding players of the National League in 1933 in Chicago. It was a promotional idea of Arch Ward, the sports editor of *The Chicago Tribune*, to hype the Chicago World's Fair of that year—"A Century of Progress." It has been played every year but one (1945) since then, moving from major league ball park to major league ball park. For several years, the all-star starting players have been selected by the fans (rather than by a committee or the two managers), except for the pitchers, who are selected by the managers. The managers of the two teams are the same managers who faced each other in the previous World Series. For four years (1959–1962), probably to make more money from the games, two games were held each year but that proved disruptive to the schedule.

1933—American, 4–2

1934—American, 9–7

1935—American, 4–1

1936—National, 4–3

1937—American, 8–3

1938—National, 4–1

1939—American, 3–1

1940—National, 4–0

1941—American, 7–5

1942—American, 3–1

1943—American, 5–3

1944—National, 7–1

1945—No Game

1946—American, 12–0

1947—American, 2–1

1948—American, 5–2

1949—American, 11–7

1950—National, 4–3

1951—National, 8–3

1952—National, 3–2 (five innings, rain)

1953—National, 5–1

1954—American, 11–9

1955—National, 6–5 (12 innings)

1956—National, 7–3

1957—American, 6–5

1958—American, 4–3

1959—American, 5–3
   National, 5–4

1960—National, 6–0
   National, 5–3

1961—National, 5–4 Tie, 1–1 (nine innings, rain)

1962—American, 9–4
   National, 3–1

1963—National, 5–3

1964—National, 7–4

1965—National, 6–5

1966—National, 2–1 (10 innings)

1967—National, 2–1 (15 innings)

1968—National, 1–0

1969—National, 9–3

1970—National, 5–4

1971—American, 6–4

1972—National, 4–3

1973—National, 7–1

1974—National, 7–2

1975—National, 6–3

1976—National, 7–1

1977—National, 7–5

1978—National, 7–3

1979—National, 7–6

1980—National, 4–2

1981—National, 5–4

1982—National, 4–1

1983—American, 13–3

1984—National, 3–1

1985—National, 6–1

1986—American, 3–2

1987—National, 2–1 (13 innings)

1988—American, 2–1

1989—American, 5–3

1990—American, 2–0

1991—American, 4–2

1992—American, 13–6

ALL-STAR MVPs

1962—**Leon Wagner,** LF, Los Angeles Angels (first game)
Maury Wills, SS, Los Angeles Dodgers (second game)

1963—**Willie Mays,** CF, San Francisco Giants

1964—**John Callison,** RF, Philadelphia Phillies

1965—**Juan Marichal,** P, San Francisco Giants

1966—**Brooks Robinson,** 3B, Baltimore Orioles

1967—**Tony Perez,** 3B, Cincinnati Reds

1968—**Willie Mays,** CF, San Francisco Giants

1969—**Willie McCovey,** 1B, San Francisco Giants

1970—**Carl Yastrzemski,** 1B, Boston Red Sox

1971—**Frank Robinson,** RF, Baltimore Orioles

1972—**Joe Morgan,** 2B, Cincinnati Reds

1973—**Bobby Bonds,** RF, San Francisco Giants

1974—**Steve Garvey,** 1B, Los Angeles Dodgers

1975—**Bill Madlock,** 3B, Chicago Cubs (tie)
Jon Matlack, P, New York Mets

1976—**George Foster,** LF, Cincinnati Reds

1977—**Don Sutton,** P, Los Angeles Dodgers

1978—**Steve Garvey,** 1B, Los Angeles Dodgers

1979—**Dave Parker,** RF, Pittsburgh Pirates

1980—**Ken Griffey, Sr.,** RF, Cincinnati Reds

1981—**Gary Carter,** C, Montreal Expos

1982—**Dave Concepcion,** SS, Cincinnati Reds

1983—**Fred Lynn,** CF, California Angels

1984—**Gary Carter,** C, Montreal Expos

1985—**LaMarr Hoyt,** P, San Diego Padres

1986—**Roger Clemens,** P, Boston Red Sox

1987—**Tim Raines,** LF, Montreal Expos

1988—**Terry Steinbach,** C, Oakland A's

1989—**Bo Jackson,** LF, Kansas City Royals

1990—**Julio Franco,** 2B, Texas Rangers

1991—**Cal Ripken, Jr.,** SS, Baltimore Orioles

1992—**Ken Griffey, Jr.,** CF, Seattle Mariners

Firsts and Lasts

Everything has a beginning and an end. Here are some of the major appearances and disappearances in the world of baseball.

Firsts

1834—The first instructional book to include baseball, *The Book of Sports,* was published.

September 23, 1845—The first baseball club, the amateur Knickerbocker Base Ball Club, was founded in New York.

April 22, 1876—The first National League game was played in Philadelphia at a diamond at 25th and Jefferson Streets. The Boston Red Stockings beat the Philadelphia Athletics, 6–5, in front of 3,000 fans. Because it was the premiere major league game. There were many major league firsts:

○ Philadelphia shortstop Davy Force had the first assist.

○ A Philadelphia first baseman made the first putout.

○ Boston center fielder Jim O'Rourke had the first hit, a single.

○ Boston's Tim McGinley scored the first run on a long fly ball by Jack Manning in the second inning.

○ Philadelphia third baseman Levi Meyerle hit the first double in the first inning.

April 24, 1876—Levi Meyerle hit the first major league triple.

May 2, 1876—Second baseman Ross Barnes of the Chicago White Stockings (later the Cubs) hit the first major league home run, an inside-the-parker against Cincinnati.

July 15, 1876—Cardinals pitcher George Washington "Grin" Bradley pitched the first major league no-hitter against the Hartford Dark Blues.

1876—The first major league batting champion was crowned. It was second baseman Ross Barnes of the Chicago White Stockings (later the Cubs), with a .404 average.

June 2, 1883—The first night game was played in sandlot baseball in Fort Wayne, Indiana, between the Fort Wayne club and a team from Quincy, Illinois. League Park in Fort Wayne was floodlit by 17 lights of 4,000 candlepower each.

May 1, 1884—The first black players in major league baseball were two brothers, Moses Fleetwood Walker and Wilberforce Welday Walker. They took the field for Toledo of the American Association, which was then considered a major league.

1884—The first ladies' day game is held by the New York Giants.

1885—The Chicago White Stockings (later the Cubs) were the first major league team to go south for spring training—to Hot Springs, Arkansas.

April 17, 1892—The first Sunday game in major league history was played. Cincinnati beat St. Louis, 5–1.

June 6, 1892—Benjamin Harrison was the first president of the United States to see a professional baseball game. He watched Cincinnati beat Washington (D. C.), 7–4 in 11 innings.

April 24, 1901—The first American League game in history was played. The Chicago White Sox beat the Cleveland Bronchos (later the Indians), 8-2, in one hour and 30 minutes in front of 14,000 fans at the Chicago Cricket Club. Three other games were scheduled, but all of them were rained out.

July 19, 1904—Cleveland shortstop Neal Ball pulled off the first unassisted triple play in major league history.

April 14, 1910—William Howard Taft became the first president of the United States to throw out the first ball of the season. The game was in Washington, and there were 12,226 fans in the ball park.

June 9, 1914—Shortstop Honus Wagner of the Pirates became the first major league player to get 3,000 base hits.

September 24, 1916—Marty Kavanaugh of the Indians hit the first major league pinch-hit grand slam homer in a 5–3 triumph over the Red Sox. The ball rolled through a hole in the fence and could not be recovered in time.

June, 1917—Catcher Hank Gowdy of the Boston Braves became the first major leaguer to volunteer for the armed forces in World War I.

August 5, 1921—Pittsburgh radio station KDKA provided its listeners with the first broadcast of a major league game. The Pirates beat the Phillies, 8-5, in Philadelphia, and the announcer was Harold Arlen.

June 1, 1925—Lou Gehrig pinch hit for shortstop Pee Wee Wanninger in the eighth inning and replaced Wally Pipp at first base to begin his 2,130 consecutive game record. The Senators beat the Yanks, 5–3.

1927—The Yankees became the first club to spend the entire season in first place.

April 28, 1930—The first minor league night game in history was played at Independence, Missouri. Muskogee, Oklahoma beat Independence, Missouri, 13–3, in this Western Association game.

July 6, 1933—The first major league All-Star game was played at Comiskey Park in Chicago. The American League, managed by Connie Mack of the Athletics, beat the National League, managed by John McGraw of the Giants, 4–2, on Babe Ruth's two-run homer.

May 23, 1935—The first scheduled major league night game, which was to be played in Cincinnati, was postponed because of rain.

May 24, 1935—The first major league night game was played at Crosley Field in Cincinnati. The Reds beat the Phillies, 2–1, before a crowd of 25,000.

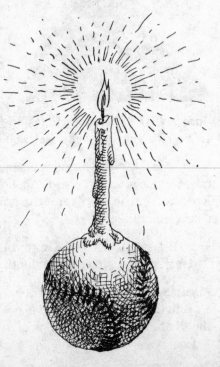

1936—The first group of major league players were elected to the Hall of Fame in Cooperstown, New York. The first roster consisted of shortstop Honus Wagner of the Pirates, right fielder Babe Ruth of the Yankees, center fielder Ty Cobb of the Tigers, pitcher Walter Johnson of the Senators, and pitcher Christy Mathewson of the Giants.

June 15, 1938—The first night game at Brooklyn's Ebbetts

Field was played. Johnny Vander Meer of the Reds pitched his second consecutive no-hitter, and Cincinnati won, 6–0.

May 16, 1939—The first American League night game was played in Philadelphia at Shibe Park.

June 27, 1939—The first night game in Cleveland's Municipal Stadium was played.

August 14, 1939—The first night game in Chicago's Comiskey Park was played.

August 26, 1939—The first televised baseball game was carried on NBC's experimental station, W2XBS. It was the first game of a doubleheader between the Reds and the Dodgers at Ebbetts Field in Brooklyn, and the Reds won. The telecast had commercials for three different products—Ivory Soap, Mobil Oil, and Wheaties breakfast cereal.

May 24, 1940—In the first night game at Sportsman's Park in St. Louis, the Browns lost to Cleveland as the Indians pitcher, Bob Feller, hit his first major league home run. He was to end his 18-year career with eight round-trippers.

May 24, 1940—The Giants played their first night game at the Polo Grounds.

June 4, 1940—The Cardinals played their first night game at Sportsman's Park in St. Louis, losing to the Dodgers, 10–1.

June 4, 1940—The Pirates played their first night game at Forbes Field.

September 6, 1940—Second baseman Johnny Lucadello of the Browns became the first player to homer both right-handed and left-handed in a single game. These two homers were his only round-trippers of the season.

May 7, 1941—Left fielder Hank Greenberg of the Tigers was the first major league player to enter the armed forces as World War II came closer to the United States.

May 26, 1941—The Senators played their first night game in Griffith Stadium in Washington.

May 11, 1946—The Braves played their first night game in Braves Field in Boston.

May 28, 1946—The Yankees played their first night game in Yankee Stadium in the Bronx, New York. The Yanks lost to the Senators, 2–1, before 49,917 fans. The first ball was thrown out by General Electric President Charles Wilson.

June 9, 1946—Mel Ott of the Giants became the first manager in major league baseball to be thrown out in both games of a doubleheader for arguing with the umpire. The Pirates won both games, 2–1 and 5–1.

1947—First baseman Jackie Robinson of the Dodgers became the first black player in modern major league history.

June 13, 1947—The Red Sox played their first night game at Fenway Park in Boston.

July 3, 1947—The Indians bought left fielder Larry Doby from the Newark Eagles of the Negro National League, making him the first black player in the American League.

July 8, 1947—In the 24th All-Star game at Wrigley Field in Chicago, Yankees pitcher Spec Shea became the first rookie pitcher to win the classic.

August 26, 1947—The Dodgers' Dan Bankhead became the first black pitcher in the major leagues. He hit a homer in his first appearance at the plate. Sent in as a relief pitcher, he gave up ten hits and six earned runs in 3⅓ innings, but did not figure in the decision as the Pirates won the game, 16–3.

October 2, 1947—Yankees catcher Yogi Berra clouted the first World Series pinch homer.

June 15, 1948—The Tigers played their first night game at Briggs Stadium in Detroit.

June 30, 1948—Bob Lemon of the Indians pitched the first night game no-hitter in the American League and beat the Tigers, 2–0.

July 11, 1950—For the first time, the All-Star game was broadcast on network television. The game was returned to Comiskey Park in Chicago, where it had begun, and the National League won 4–3, in 14 innings.

April 19, 1956—The first major league baseball game ever played in New Jersey occured at Roosevelt Stadium in Jersey City as the Dodgers beat the Phillies, 5–4, in ten innings.

June 13, 1957—Left fielder Ted Williams of the Red Sox hit three home runs and drove in five runs as Boston beat the Indians, 9–3.

This was the first time an American League player had two three-homer games in a single season.

May 15, 1960—Chicago Cubs pitcher Don Cardwell became the first hurler to throw a no-hitter in his first start after being traded. He had just come from the Phillies. The final score of the game was 4–0 in favor of the Cubs.

May 27, 1960—The first "big mitt" used to catch knuckleball pitches was used by Baltimore's Clint Courtney, who caught for Wilhelm. The mitt, designed by baseball executive and former catcher Paul Richards, was 50 percent larger than the standard mitt. The Orioles beat the Yankees, 3–2.

1962—The first Sunday night game in baseball history was played in Houston, and the Colt 45s (later the Astros) beat the Giants, 3–0. Permission to build the Astrodome was granted because of the excessive heat in Houston during the day—this was before the Astrodome was built.

June 22, 1962—Left fielder Boog Powell of the Orioles became the first batter to hit a home run over the center field hedge at Baltimore's Memorial Stadium. It was a 469-foot shot off pitcher Don Schwall of the Red Sox.

1966—Emmett Littleton Ashford became the first black umpire in modern major league baseball. He was hired by the American League.

July 9, 1968—The first indoor All-Star game was played in the Houston Astrodome. It was also the first such contest to be decided by a 1–0 score, as the National League beat the American League.

October 13, 1971—The first World Series night game was played in Pittsburgh, and the Pirates beat the Orioles, 4–3.

September 7, 1974—One of Angels pitcher Nolan Ryan's pitches was officially clocked at 100.8 miles per hour in a game against the White Sox. He became the first player to break the 100-mph barrier.

1975—Frank Robinson became the first black manager in the major leagues as he took over the Indians.

1978—The Dodgers were the first team to draw more than three million fans, setting an attendance record of 3,347,845.

1981—Frank Robinson became the first black manager in the National League, taking over the Giants.

August 20, 1985—Pitcher Dwight Gooden of the Mets struck out 16 batters in a 3–0 victory over San Francisco, becoming the first National League pitcher to strike out 200 or more batters in each of his first two years. He was to extend his record to three years in 1986.

1987—Orioles manager Cal Ripken, Sr. became the first father ever to manage two sons (Cal, Jr. and Billy) simultaneously in the major leagues.

August 8, 1988—The first scheduled night game at Wrigley Field in Chicago was rained out in the bottom of the fourth inning with the Cubs ahead, 3–1.

August 9, 1988—The first complete night game at Wrigley Field in Chicago ended with the Cubs beating the Mets, 6–4.

1988—José Canseco became the first major leaguer to steal 40 bases and hit 40 home runs in the same season.

1989—Mark McGwire of the A's became the first player to hit 30 or more home runs in each of his first four years in the major leagues.

1990—George Brett of the Royals became the first man in major league history to win a batting title in three separate decades (1976: .333; 1980: .390; 1990: .329).

1990—Willie McGee became the first man to win a batting title in one league while playing in another. By August, while he was with the Cardinals, his batting average was .335, and that held up for the National League title, even though he had been traded to the A's.

1990—Barry Bonds of the Pirates became the first man to drive in 100 runs, score 100 runs, hit 30 home runs, and steal 50 bases while batting .300.

August 19, 1992—When second baseman Bret Boone played his first major league game for the Seattle Mariners, he went one for three. But more than that, he was the first third-generation major leaguer. His grandfather, Ray Boone, was an infielder for the Indians and the Tigers for 13 years. His father, Bob Boone, was a catcher for the Phillies, Angels, and Royals for 18 years.

October 14, 1992—Cito Gaston of the Toronto Blue Jays became the first black manager to win a league pennant, and went on to win the World Series.

Lasts

And now for some real nostalgia:

October 15, 1892—Charles Leander "Bumpus" Jones of Cincinnati beat Pittsburgh, 7–1, in the last no-hitter pitched from a distance of 50 feet.

September 4, 1916—The pitching legends, Christy Mathewson of the Giants and Mordecai "Three-Finger" Brown of the Cubs, both to become Hall of Famers, faced each other. It was to be the last game for them both.

September 22, 1911—Cy Young, at age 44, beat the Pirates, 1–0, for his 511th and last victory, setting a record for total wins that still stands.

October 2, 1920—The Reds and Pirates played the last major league triple header.

1933—On the last day of the season, Babe Ruth pitched his last game—for the Yankees. He went the distance to win, 6–5.

1934—This was the last year in which all the major league baseball games were played in the daytime.

May 25, 1935—Babe Ruth, now playing for the Boston Braves, hit the last three home runs of his career in Pittsburgh.

May 30, 1935—Babe Ruth played his last baseball game.

April 30, 1939—Lou Gehrig played his last baseball game.

July 25, 1941—Pitcher Lefty Grove, now with the Red Sox, won his 300th and last game by beating the Indians, 10–6.

1948—Indian shortstop Lou Boudreau became the last player-manager to win a pennant.

October 1, 1950—After 50 years managing the Philadelphia Athletics, Connie Mack piloted his last game.

September 21, 1952—Only 8,822 fans saw the last game at Braves Field in Boston before the Braves move to Milwaukee.

September 24, 1957—Dodger pitcher Danny McDevitt shut out the Pirates, 3–0, in the Dodger's last game in Ebbetts Field before they moved to Los Angeles.

September 30, 1957—The Giants lost to the Pirates in their last game in the Polo Grounds before they moved to San Francisco.

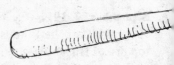

1959—The Boston Red Sox became the last major league team to sign a black player, second baseman Pumpsie Green.

September 18, 1963—The Mets lost their last game in the Polo Grounds to the Phillies, 5–1. Only 1,752 fans showed up for the final major league game to be played at that stadium. In 1964, the Mets moved to the brand-new Shea Stadium.

September 29, 1963—Left fielder Stan Musial of the Cardinals got the last hit of his career, number 3,630.

May 8, 1966—The Cardinals played their last game in the old Busch Stadium, losing, 10–5, to the Giants.

May 11, 1971—Steve Dunning of the Indians hit the last grand slam home run by an American League pitcher (before the designated hitter rule) off Diego Segui of the A's.

September 30, 1972—Right fielder Roberto Clemente of the Pirates doubled off Mets pitcher Jon Matlack for his 3,000th and last hit.

November 2, 1972—Shortstop Freddie Parent of the old Boston Somersets (later the Red Sox), the last survivor of the first World Series in 1903, died at the age of 96.

July 20, 1976—Designated hitter Hank Aaron of the Brewers hit his last home run—number 755—off Dick Drago of the A's.

The Teams

Major league baseball today consists of 26 teams—12 in the National League and 14 in the American League. But it was not always so. For example, the National League in 1876, its first year, consisted of eight teams—Chicago, St. Louis, Hartford (Connecticut), Boston, Louisville (Kentucky), New York, Philadelphia, and Cincinnati. Over the years, teams came and teams went.

At one time or another, there were National League clubs in Providence (Rhode Island), Indianapolis (Indiana), Milwaukee (Wisconsin), Buffalo (New York), Cleveland (Ohio), Syracuse (New York), Troy (New York), Worcester (Massachusetts), Detroit (Michigan), Kansas City (Missouri), Washington (D.C.), and Baltimore (Maryland). But who remembers the Louisville Grays, the Louisville Colonels, the Hartford Dark Blues (who played their 1877 home games in Brooklyn), the Cleveland Spiders, the Troy Haymakers, the Buffalo Bisons, the Providence Grays, or the Detroit Wolverines? When the American League was formed in 1901, Baltimore, Washington, and Cleveland left the National League to join it.

But now the number of teams seems relatively stable. Here are facts on the present major league teams.

National League

The address of the National League Office is 350 Park Avenue, New York, NY 10022.

ATLANTA BRAVES 521 Capitol Ave., SW, Atlanta, GA 30312. The Braves play their home games in Atlanta-Fulton Country Stadium, which seats 52,003. The home run distances in left, center, and right fields are 330, 402, and 330 feet, and it has natural grass.

The team made its debut in the National League in 1876 as the Boston Red Stockings. The team's name changed several times from 1883 to 1952. They were the Boston Beaneaters (1883–1906), the Boston Doves (1907–1908), the Boston Pilgrims (1909–1911), the Boston Braves (1912–1935), the Boston Bees (1936–1940), and the Boston Braves again (1941–1952).

In 1953, the Braves moved to Milwaukee, where they played in Milwaukee County Stadium, which today is the home of the Brewers. That year, in the first 13 games of the new season, they surpassed their total 1952 attendance in Boston of 281,278. In 1966, the Braves' owners stunned the baseball world by selling the team to broadcasting magnate Ted Turner, who moved them to Atlanta, where they have been ever since.

CHICAGO CUBS Wrigley Field, Chicago, IL 60613. The Cubs play their homes games in Wrigley Field, which seats 38,710. Finally, in 1988, it was the last ball park to install lights for night games. The stadium's home run distances in left, center, and right fields are 355, 400, and 353 feet, and it has natural grass.

The Chicago team, known as the White Stockings, won the first National League pennant in 1876. The name was changed to the Cubs in 1901.

In 1914, Weeghman Park, then seating only 14,000, was built at a cost of $250,000 for the Chicago Whales of the Federal League—a league that lasted only two years. The Cubs took over Weeghman Park in 1916. In 1920, the stadium was renamed Cubs Park, and in 1926, it became Wrigley Field in honor of William Wrigley, Jr., the club's owner.

CINCINNATI REDS 100 Riverfront Stadium, Cincinnati, OH 45202. The Reds play their home games in Riverfront Stadium, opened in 1970, with its seating capacity of 52,952. The home run distances in left, center, and right fields are 330, 404, and 330 feet, and there is artificial turf.

One of the original members of the National League in 1876, the Cincinnati Redlegs were expelled from the league after the 1880 season for selling beer and playing on Sunday but were reinstated for the 1881 season. They were rechristened the Reds, but from 1944 to 1945, they called themselves the Redlegs, probably because they feared that people might think of them as being Communists. The name, Reds, came back in 1946. For many years, the club played in the old Crosley Field, which held only 29,488 fans.

COLORADO ROCKIES 1700 Broadway, Denver, CO 80290. The Rockies play their home games in Mile High Stadium, which seats 76,100. The home run distances in left, center, and right fields are 335, 423, and 370, and it has natural grass.

In 1991, Denver was granted an expansion franchise in the National League, and the Rockies began their first season in 1993.

FLORIDA MARLINS 100 NE Third Avenue, Fort Lauderdale, FL 33301. The Marlins play their games in Joe Robbie Stadium, which seats 48,000. The home run distances in left, center, and right fields are 335, 410, and 345, and it has natural grass.

In 1991, Miami was granted an expansion franchise in the National League, and the Marlins began their first season in 1993.

HOUSTON ASTROS 8400 Kirby Drive, Houston, TX 77054. The Astros play their home games in the Astrodome, the country's first indoor ball park, which seats 54,816. The home run distances in left, center, and right fields are 330, 400, and 330, and there is artificial turf, called Astroturf.

In 1962, Houston was granted an expansion franchise in the National League, and fielded a club called the Houston Colt 45s. The 45s played their games in Colt Stadium, which held only 32,601 fans. When the Astrodome was opened in 1965, the team took on a new name—the Houston Astros.

LOS ANGELES DODGERS Dodger Stadium, Los Angeles, CA 90012. The Dodgers play their home games in Dodger Stadium, which seats 56,000. Its home run distances in left, center, and right fields are 330, 395, and 330, and it has natural grass.

The team that was to become the Los Angeles Dodgers entered the National League in 1884, under the name of the Brooklyn Bridegrooms. In 1899, they were renamed the Brooklyn Superbas, a title that stuck until 1910. Because people in Brooklyn at that time often called themselves "trolley dodgers," the club became the Dodgers in 1911. For a time in the second decade of this century, they were also called the Brooklyn Robins in honor of their manager, Wilbert Robinson. For years they played ball in Ebbetts Field, a cosy park that seated 31,902.

In 1958, the team left Brooklyn and settled in Los Angeles. Their first ball park there was the Los Angeles Coliseum, which is primarily a football arena. It held 94,600 fans, but its proportions were not ideal for baseball, since the home run distances in left, center, and right fields were 251, 420, and 333 feet.

MONTREAL EXPOS PO Box 500, Station M, Montreal, Quebec H1V 3P2, Canada. The Expos play their home games in Olympic Stadium, with its capacity of 43,739. Its home run distances in left, center, and right fields are 325, 404, and 325 feet, and it has artificial turf.

The Expos were an expansion team in 1969, the year they joined the National League. For the first few years they played in tiny Jarry Park, which seated 30,000 fans.

NEW YORK METS Shea Stadium, Flushing, NY 11368. The Mets play their home games in Shea Stadium, which seats 55,601. It has natural grass, and the home run distances in left, center, and right fields are 338, 410, and 338 feet.

The team was one of the two expansion teams admitted to the National League in 1962. They played in the old Polo Grounds in New York—the ball park that had been empty since the Giants left town—which held 55,000. When Shea Stadium was opened in 1964, the Mets played their first game there on April 17.

PHILADELPHIA PHILLIES PO Box 7575, Philadelphia, PA 19101. The Phillies play their home games in Veterans Stadium, which has a capacity of 62,382. The turf is artificial, and the home run distances in left, center, and right fields are 330, 408, and 330 feet.

The team was one of the charter members of the National League when it was formed in 1876. Known then as the Philadelphia Athletics, they changed their name to the Phillies in 1883. In 1943 and 1944, they called themselves the Blue Jays. In 1938, they moved to Shibe Park after playing for 51 years in Baker Bowl, which was a tiny bandbox of a stadium.

PITTSBURGH PIRATES Three Rivers Stadium, Pittsburgh, PA 15212. The Pirates play their home games in Three Rivers Stadium, which holds 58,727 fans. Equipped with artificial turf, its home run distances in left, center, and right field are 335, 400, and 335 feet. Pittsburgh joined the National League in 1882, and they were to be the losing team in the first World Series in 1903—losing to Boston, five games to three. For years they played in the old Forbes Field, which seated 35,000. The new Three Rivers Stadium was opened in 1970.

ST. LOUIS CARDINALS Busch Stadium, St. Louis, MO 63102. The Cardinals play their home games in Busch Stadium, which seats 56,227 fans. The home run distances in left, center, and right fields are 330, 414, and 330 feet, and it has artificial turf. The club started play in the National League in 1882 when they were known as the Brown Stockings or the Browns. The name was changed to the Cardinals in 1889. For years they shared old Sportsman's Park, which could accommodate 30,490 people, with the St. Louis Browns of the American League. After the Cards were bought by August Busch, the beer baron, the park's name was changed to Busch Stadium. The new Busch Stadium was opened in 1966.

SAN DIEGO PADRES 9449 Friars Road, San Diego, CA 92108. The Padres play their home games in Jack Murphy Stadium, which seats 59,022. Its home run distances in left, center, and right fields are 327, 405, and 327, and it has natural grass. The team joined the National League in 1969 as an expansion team.

SAN FRANCISCO GIANTS Candlestick Park, San Francisco, CA 94124. Candlestick Park, where the Giants play their home games, can accommodate 58,000 people. Its home run distances in left, center, and right fields are 335, 400, and 330 feet, and it has natural grass.

The franchise entered the National League in 1876, the first year of the league, as the New York Giants. For years they played in the Polo Grounds in New York, which held 55,000 fans. But in 1957 it was announced that they were moving to San Francisco, and they began play there in 1958. The Giants took over a former minor league park, the old Seals Stadium (capacity: 22,900), and then moved to the new Candlestick Park.

American League

The address of the American League Office is 350 Park Avenue, New York, NY 10022.

BALTIMORE ORIOLES Oriole Park at Camden Yards, 333 West Camden St., Baltimore, MD 21201. The Orioles play their home games in Oriole Park at Camden Yards, which has a capacity of 48,041. The home run distances in left, center, and right fields are 335, 400, and 319, and it has natural grass.

The Orioles began their American League history in 1902 as the St. Louis Browns. For years they shared the old Sportsman's Park in St. Louis with the Cardinals of the National League. But the team was never a success, and in 1954 they moved to Baltimore and changed their name to the Orioles, playing in Memorial Stadium (capacity 53,371) until 1992, when they moved to their new stadium.

BOSTON RED SOX 24 Yawkey Way, Boston, MA 02215. The Sox play their home games in the fine old stadium known as Fenway Park, opened in 1912. The park seats 33,583, its surface is natural grass, and its home run distances in left, center, and right fields are 315, 420, and 302 feet.

The team was a charter member of the American League when it was formed in 1901, and was known as the Boston Somersets until 1904, and then as the Boston Puritans until 1906.

CALIFORNIA ANGELS Anaheim Stadium, Anaheim, CA 92806. The Angels play their home games in Anaheim Stadium, with its seating capacity of 64,593. Its home run distances in left, center, and right fields are 333, 404, and 333 feet, and it has natural grass.

The team made its debut in 1961 as an expansion team in the American League. At that time it was called the Los Angeles Angels, and played in Los Angeles' minor league park, Wrigley Field, which could accommodate 20,543. Then the club moved to Chavez Ravine Stadium in Los Angeles, which could seat 56,000. The team moved south to Anaheim in 1966, and became the California Angels.

CHICAGO WHITE SOX 333 West 35th Street, Chicago, IL 60616. The Sox play their home games in Comiskey Park, which seats 44,229. Its home run distances in left, center, and right fields are 347, 400, and 347, and it has natural grass.

Formerly, the club played in the old Comiskey Park, which opened in 1910 as White Sox Park, with its capacity of 44,087. The team, which moved into the new stadium in 1991, was a charter member of the American League in 1901, and it won the first American League pennant.

CLEVELAND INDIANS Cleveland Stadium, Cleveland, OH 44114. The Indians play their home games in Cleveland Stadium, which opened in 1932. The park holds 74,483—the largest capacity in the major leagues. Its home run distances in left, center, and right fields are 320, 415, and 320 feet, and it has natural grass.

Oddly enough, the Cleveland team began as the Cleveland Spiders in the National League, but switched to the American League when that circuit was formed in 1901. The team had a little trouble with names for a while—they were called the Cleveland Bronchos (1901), the Cleveland Blues (1902–1904), the Cleveland Naps (1905–1911), and the Cleveland Molly McGuires (1912–1914), before becoming the Cleveland Indians in 1915.

DETROIT TIGERS Tiger Stadium, Detroit, MI 48216. The Tigers play their home games in Tiger Stadium, which has a seating capacity of 52,416. It has natural grass, and its home run distances in left, center, and right fields are 340, 440, and 325 feet.

The team was in at the formation of the American League in 1901. For years it played in the old Bennett Field before Briggs Stadium, later renamed Tiger Stadium, was built in 1912.

KANSAS CITY ROYALS P.O. Box 419969, Kansas City, MO 64141. The Royals play their home games in Royals Stadium, which holds 40,625 fans. It has artificial turf, and the home run distances in left, center, and right fields are 330, 410, and 330 feet. The team came into being as an expansion club in the American League in 1969.

MILWAUKEE BREWERS Milwaukee County Stadium, Milwaukee, WI 53214. The Brewers play their home games in Milwaukee County Stadium, which has a seating capacity of 53,192. The home run distances in left, center, and right fields are 315, 402, and 315 feet, and it has natural grass.

In 1969, Seattle fielded an expansion club in the American League—the Seattle Pilots. The team lasted but one year before it moved to Milwaukee, taking the field as the Brewers in 1970.

MINNESOTA TWINS 501 Chicago Avenue South, Minneapolis, MN 55415. The Twins play their home games in the Hubert H. Humphrey Metrodome in Bloomington, Minnesota, which holds 55,883 people. Its home run distances in left, center, and right fields are 343, 408, and 327 feet, and it has artificial turf.

The Twins' ancestors, the Washington Senators, were charter members of the American League when the League was founded in 1901. But in 1961, after years of falling attendance, the team moved to Minnesota and changed its name to the Twins.

NEW YORK YANKEES Yankee Stadium, The Bronx, NY 10451. The Yankees play their home games in Yankee Stadium, with its seating capacity of 57,545. The stadium has natural grass, and its home run distances in left, center, and right fields are 318, 408, and 314 feet.

In 1892, a team called the Baltimore Orioles joined the National League, where it remained until the organization of the American

League, when it skipped to the junior circuit. The team stayed in Baltimore until it moved to New York to open the 1903 season. The New York team called itself the Highlanders until 1912, when the name was changed to the Yankees. For many years it shared the Polo Grounds with the Giants, until Yankee Stadium was opened in 1923.

OAKLAND A'S Oakland Coliseum, Oakland, CA 94621. The A's play their home games in Oakland Alameda County Coliseum, which can seat 47,313. The stadium has natural grass, and its home run distances in left, center, and right fields are 330, 400, and 330 feet.

The team began in Philadelphia as the Philadelphia Athletics—one of the charter members of the American League in 1901. Toward the end of their stay in Philadelphia, they played in Connie Mack Stadium, which held 33,233 fans. But the fans didn't show up because of the team's poor record, and it was moved to Kansas City to become the Kansas City Athletics in 1955. While there, the A's played in Municipal Stadium, with its seating capacity of 32,561. In 1968, the team opened the season in Oakland, California, as the Oakland A's.

SEATTLE MARINERS PO Box 4100, Seattle, WA 98104. The Mariners appear at the Kingdome, which holds 57,748 fans. It has artificial turf, and its home run distances in left, center, and right fields are 331, 405, and 312 feet. The team was formed as an expansion club in the American League to open the 1977 season.

TEXAS RANGERS 1250 E. Copeland Road, Arlington, TX 76011. The Rangers play their home games in Arlington Stadium, which can seat 43,521. It has natural grass, and the home run distances in left, center, and right fields are 330, 400, and 330 feet.

When the Washington Senators left the District of Columbia for Minnesota after the 1960 season, they were immediately granted an American League expansion franchise. The Minnesota team was also called the Senators. But after three unsuccessful seasons, the team left for Texas, where it opened the 1972 season as the Texas Rangers.

TORONTO BLUE JAYS 300 Bremner Blvd., Toronto, Ontario M5V 3B3, Canada. The Blue Jays play their home games in Skydome, which has a seating capacity of 50,516. It has artificial Astroturf, and its home run distances in left, center, and right fields are 328, 400, and 328 feet. Toronto first took the field in 1977, after the city had received an expansion team franchise from the American League.

Spring Training

All major league ball clubs have spring training either in Florida or Arizona. Here are the locations.

NATIONAL LEAGUE

Atlanta Braves—Municipal Stadium, West Palm Beach, FL

Chicago Cubs—Ho Ho Ham Park, Mesa, AZ

Cincinnati Reds—Reds Spring Training Complex, Plant City, FL

Denver Rockies—Cocoa Expo, Cocoa, FL

Florida Marlins—Hi Corbett Field, Tucson, AZ

Houston Astros—Osceola County Stadium, Kissimmee, FL

Los Angeles Dodgers—Holman Stadium, Vero Beach, FL

Montreal Expos—Municipal Stadium, West Palm Beach, FL

New York Mets—St. Lucie County Sports Complex, Port St. Lucie, Fl

Philadelphia Phillies—Jack Russell Stadium, Clearwater, FL

Pittsburgh Pirates—McKechnie Field, Bradenton, FL

St. Louis Cardinals—Al Lang Stadium, St. Petersburg, FL

San Diego Padres—Desert Sun
Stadium, Yuma, AZ

San Francisco Giants—Scottsdale Stadium, Scottsdale,
AZ

AMERICAN LEAGUE

Baltimore Orioles—for the
1993 season: Twin Lake
Park, Sarasota, FL (February
20–March 5); Al Lang Sta-
dium, St. Petersburg, FL
(March 6–April 1)

Boston Red Sox—Red Sox Stadium, Ft. Myers, FL

California Angels—Gene Autry
Park, Mesa, AZ

Chicago White Sox—Ed Smith
Stadium, Sarasota, FL

Cleveland Indians—Chain O'
Lakes Complex, Winter Ha-
ven, FL

Detroit Tigers—Joker Merchant
Stadium, Lakeland, FL

Kansas City Royals—Baseball
City Sports Complex, Davenport, FL

Milwaukee Brewers—Compa-
dre Stadium, Chandler, AZ

Minnesota Twins—Lee County
Stadium, Ft. Myers, FL

New York Yankees—Fort Lauderdale Stadium, Fort Lauderdale, FL

Oakland Athletics—Phoenix
Municipal Stadium, Phoenix,
AZ

Seattle Mariners—Tempe Dia-
blo Stadium, Tempe, AZ

Texas Rangers—Charlotte
County Stadium, Port Charlotte, FL

Toronto Blue Jays—Dunedin
Stadium at Grant Field,
Dunedin, FL

What Did He Say?

Baseball people throughout history have always had something to say. More than in any other sport, baseball players, managers, umpires, writers, and executives have felt called upon to offer their reading or listening public some pithy comments, flaky observations, and probing musings. Here are a few gems.

Managers

SPARKY ANDERSON
Manager of the Reds (1970–1978) and the Tigers (1979–)

"My biggest job as manager is that I don't trip the players going down the runway."

YOGI BERRA
Hall of Fame catcher and manager of the Yankees (1964), the Mets (1972–1975), and the Yankees again (1984–1985)

"I can't think and hit at the same time." (Berra struck out looking after being told to think when he was at bat.)

After facing Dodgers pitcher Sandy Koufax in the 1963 World Series: "I can see how he won 25 games. What I don't understand is how he lost five."

"You've got to be very careful if you don't know where you're going, because you might not get there."

Speaking about the shortening of the days in the autumn: "It gets late early out there."

"If people don't want to come to the ball park, how are you going to stop them?"

Speaking of the game of baseball: "It's not over till it's over."

After a loss: "We made too many wrong mistakes."

On playing the game: "You observe a lot by watching."

When taking on the job of managing the Yankees for the first time: "My big problem as manager will be to see if I can manage."

After a state dinner: "How could you get a conversation started in there? Everybody was talking too much."

When an elderly woman told him after a game that he looked "mighty cool today": "Thank you, ma'am. You don't look so hot yourself."

ALVIN DARK

Manager of the Giants (1961–1964), the Kansas City A's (1966–1967), the Indians (1968–1971), the Oakland A's (1974–1975), and the Padres (1977)

"The Lord taught me to love everybody, but the last ones I learned to love were the sportswriters."

LEO DUROCHER

Manager of the Dodgers (1939–1946, 1948), the Giants (1948–1955), the Cubs (1966–1972), and the Astros (1972–1973)

"You don't save a pitcher for tomorrow. Tomorrow it may rain."

"Nice guys finish last."

TOMMY LASORDA

Manager of the Dodgers (1976–)

Describing his 43-year-old pitcher: "We've timed Don Sutton's fastball at 92 miles an hour—46 going in to [catcher] Rick Dempsey, 46 coming back."

CONNIE MACK

Manager of the Pirates (1894–1896) and the Athletics (1901–1950)

On his retirement after 50 years as Philadelphia manager: "I am not quitting because I am too old. I am quitting because I think the people want me to quit."

MARTY MARION

Manager of the Cardinals (1951), the Browns (1952–1953), and the White Sox (1954–1956)

"I'd say that [Mickey] Mantle today is the greatest player in either league. No weaknesses? Let's see—uh, yes. There's one thing he can't do very well. He can't throw left-handed." (Mantle is right-handed.)

DANNY OZARK

Manager of the Phillies (1973–1979) and the Giants (1984)

About an inferior ballplayer: "His limitations are limitless."

After a losing streak: "Even Napoleon had his Watergate."

WILBERT ROBINSON

Manager of the Orioles (1902) and the Dodgers (1914–1931)

After three Dodgers ended up on third base at the same time, resulting in a triple play: "Leave them alone. It's the first time they've been together all season."

PETE ROSE

Manager of the Reds (1984–1989)

"There is one more important reason that I slide [into base] head first. It gets my picture in the newspaper."

On one of his few regrets: "I wish there was some way I could have gotten a college education. I'm thinking about buying a college, though."

On the appointment of Bart Giamatti, the president of Yale University, as president of the National League: "He's an intellectual from Yale, but he's very intelligent."

CASEY STENGEL

Manager of the Dodgers (1934–1936), the Braves (1938–1943), the Yankees (1949–1960), and the Mets (1962–1965)

"I was not successful as a ballplayer, as it was a game of skill."

"Pitchers are selfish men."

"The secret to managing is to keep the five guys who hate you away from the five guys who are undecided."

Commenting on his Mets' 40–120 season in their first year in the National League: "I won with this club what I used to lose."

During the first year managing the Mets: "Can't anybody here play this game?"

DON ZIMMER

Manager of the Padres (1972–1973), the Red Sox (1976–1980), the Rangers (1981–1982), and the Cubs (1989–1991)

After a road trip in which the Cubs finished with four wins and four losses: "It just as easily could have gone the other way."

Players

ERNIE BANKS

Hall of Fame Cub infielder

"It's a beautiful day—let's play two."

TERRY FRANCONA

First baseman
Comment at the Hall of Fame Game in Cooperstown in 1988: "I wonder how many more 10 RBI seasons I need to get back here."

WILLIE KEELER

Hall of Fame right fielder
On his batting technique: "Hit 'em where they ain't."

RALPH KINER

Hall of Fame slugging left fielder
"Home run hitters drive Cadillacs, singles hitters drive Fords."

STAN MUSIAL

Hall of Fame outfielder-first baseman
On his position as senior vice-president of the Cardinals: "I have a darn good job, but please don't ask me what I do."

GRAIG NETTLES

Former Yankee third baseman
"When I was a little boy, I wanted to be a baseball player and join a circus. With the Yankees, I've accomplished both."

GERALD PERRY

Braves' first baseman
After being told that the Braves drew only 848,089 fans in 1988: "This would have been a good year to paint the seats."

BABE RUTH

Hall of Fame slugger

After it was pointed out that he earned more than President Herbert Hoover in 1931: "Well, I had a better year."

On his system for hitting home runs: "All I can tell 'em is I pick a good one and sock it. I get back to the dugout and they ask me what it was I hit and I tell 'em I don't know except it looked good."

DICK TWEED

Later a baseball scout

Describing his only major league at bat: "I struck out, but I went down taking good cuts."

Pitchers

JIM BOUTON

Former pitcher

On why baseball is better than football: "Baseball is played by normal human beings. You don't have to weigh 270 pounds or bench press the team bus."

"Baseball players are smarter than football players. How often do you see a baseball team penalized for having too many players on the field?"

"Baseball sets a better example for kids. When the announcers say that a player 'likes to hit,' they're not talking about assault and battery."

DOCK ELLIS

Former Pittsburgh pitcher

"Good pitching beats good hitting—and vice versa."

DIZZY DEAN

Hall of Fame pitcher

"It's only bragging when you say you're going to do something and then can't do it."

After he won a three-hit game in a doubleheader and his brother,

Daffy, pitched a no-hitter in the second game: "If I'd known Paul was going to do that, I'd have pitched a no-hitter, too."

As a baseball broadcaster, when he was told that his syntax greatly distressed educators: "Sin tax? Are them jokers down in Washington puttin' a tax on that, too?"

Broadcasting a steal: "They woulda had him at second, but he slud."

NED GARVER

The star pitcher for the fanless Browns
"The crowd didn't boo us because we had them outnumbered."

LEFTY GOMEZ

Hall of Fame pitcher
When asked by his catcher what he wanted to throw slugger Jimmie Foxx "To tell you the truth, Bill [Dickey], I don't want to throw him anything at all."

"I'd rather be lucky than good."

OREL HERSHISER

Dodger pitcher
After winning the Cy Young Award in 1988: "I worked hard with the talent I was given and everything just worked out perfect. My career will go downhill from here."

TUG MCGRAW

Mets relief pitcher

When the team was in last place on August 30, 1973: "Ya gotta believe!" (The Mets won 20 of their last 28 games and won the National League pennant).

SATCHEL PAIGE

Hall of Fame pitcher

"You win a few, you lose a few. Some are rained out. But you got to dress for all of them."

Paige was noted for his longevity; his six steps to eternal youth:

1. Avoid fried meats, which angry up the blood.
2. If your stomach disputes you, lie down and pacify it with cool thoughts.
3. Keep the juices flowing by jangling around gently as you move.
4. Go very light on the vices, such as carrying on in society. The social rumble ain't restful.
5. Avoid running at all times.
6. Don't look back. Something might be gaining on you.

ROBIN ROBERTS

Former Phillies pitcher

"I had a high fastball, and I either overpowered them or they overpowered me."

CURT SIMMONS

Former pitcher

On throwing a fastball past Henry Aaron: "It's like trying to sneak the sunrise past a rooster."

DON SUTTON

Dodger pitcher

After being sent to the minors for conditioning and pitching into the seventh inning for the first time in months: "I finally got to hear 'Take Me Out to the Ball Game.'"

Executives

HARRY FRAZEE

Owner of the Red Sox in 1919

After selling Babe Ruth to the Yankees: "Ruth had become simply impossible, and the Boston club could no longer put up with his eccentricities. I think the Yankees are taking a gamble."

JIM FREY

General manager of the Cubs

About installing lights at Wrigley Field: "Would someone tell me when tradition starts? What do they want us to do, play without gloves because they didn't use them in the nineteenth century?"

CLARK GRIFFITH

Former executive

On installing lights at Cincinnati's Crosley Field in 1935: "There is no chance of night baseball ever becoming popular in the bigger cities because high-class baseball cannot be played under artificial lights."

KENESAW MOUNTAIN LANDIS

First commissioner of baseball

To Yankee owner, Colonel Jacob Ruppert, after Ruppert complained that Giant outfielder Casey Stengel had thumbed his nose at him after he had hit a home run to beat the Yankees in the 1923 World Series: "When a man hits a home run to win a World Series game, he is entitled to a certain amount of exuberance. Especially if he's Casey Stengel."

BRANCH RICKEY

Former general manager
"It's better to get rid of a player too soon than too late."

KEN SHEPARD

General manager of the minor league Geneva, New York, Cubs
After promising to sleep in the stadium press box until his club won (they went on to lose 18 straight games): "Every day I get crankier and crankier. There's no air conditioning up there. The mosquitoes are terrible. I want to go home."

Writers

WARREN BROWN

Sportswriter for the Chicago Tribune
On the 1945 World Series between the Cubs and the Tigers, when most of the baseball stars were in the armed forces: "I don't think either of them can win."

HENRY CHADWICK

Baseball editor of the New York Clipper *in 1876*
"Say what you will, gentlemen of the league, you must come down in your price; you must come down to the twenty-five cent admission fee; and you must proportionately lower your salaries. One thousand dollars for seven months of such services as the professional ball player is called upon to perform, even when he is not indisposed, is amply sufficient."

JAMES MICHENER

Novelist (Hawaii, Centennial)
"Young man, when you root for the Phillies, you acquire a sense of tragedy."

MARK TWAIN

Nineteenth-century novelist (The Adventures of Tom Sawyer, The Adventures of Huckleberry Finn)

"[Baseball is] the very symbol, the outward and visible expression of the drive and push and rush and struggle of the raging, tearing, booming nineteenth century."

Miscellaneous Quotes

ANONYMOUS ADVERTISEMENT

For the Cal Ripken Baseball School

As the Orioles were going through 21 straight losses at the beginning of the 1988 season: "Learn to play baseball the Oriole way."

RON LUCIANO

Former American League umpire

On the spitball: "One of the few things about baseball that hasn't changed since the turn of the century is the fact that pitchers cheat. They break the rules. They flaunt authority. And worse, they are unsanitary about it."

On pitchers: "After much soul-searching, after much questioning, I can state without hesitation that I am against the death penalty for pitchers."

MARTIN MULL

Comedian, on why baseball is better than football

"There are fewer people named Bubba."

"The players needn't pose as college graduates."

"There is plenty of time to absorb the thought-provoking spectacle of a man in a chicken suit."

"You can wear the hat backwards."

"On a rainy day, there's a darn good chance that you might get to see an acre of land covered by rubber sheeting—if you're into that sort of thing."

FRANKLIN D. ROOSEVELT

President of the United States, 1933–1944

Answering suggestions in 1942 that baseball should be cancelled for the duration of World War II: "I honestly feel that it would be best for the country to keep baseball going."

Just Plain Trivia

In the more than 100 years since the beginning of professional major league baseball, there have been a number of unusual events. Here's a line up of little-known facts, along with some hard ball nostalgia.

Oldest and Youngest

○ On October 3, 1897, **Cap Anson** closed out a career which had begun in 1871 by hitting two home runs for the Cubs against St. Louis. He was 46, the oldest player to homer in the major leagues.

○ Outfielder **Minnie Minoso,** primarily a White Sox player, was the only man to play in the majors in four different decades—beginning in 1949 and ending in 1980.

○ **Connie Mack** managed the Philadelphia Athletics for 50 years.

○ On August 31, 1906, the Tigers, crippled by injuries, called 46-year-old **Sam Thompson** out of retirement for help in the outfield. He batted in two runs in a 5–1 victory over the Browns.

○ In 1985, **Dwight Gooden** of the Mets became the youngest pitcher, at age 21, to win 20 games.

Winners and Losers

○ **Ernie Banks** of the Chicago Cubs, although elected to the Hall of Fame and a player in 2,528 games in his 19-year career, never played in a World Series.

○ **Philadelphia** is the home of the cellar dwellers. The Athletics finished last 17 times before moving to Kansas City in 1955, and the Phillies have finished last 27 times.

○ In 1946, the **St. Louis Browns** drew only 93,000 fans, and at one game only 34 people showed up.

○ **Bill Sharman,** who played basketball for the Boston Celtics and made the Pro Basketball Hall of Fame, also played baseball, batting .286 for Fort Worth in the Texas League. He was called up to the Brooklyn Dodgers in 1951, and was sitting on their bench when he was ejected by the umpire, who had cleared the bench. Sharman never got into a game in the major leagues.

○ **Joe Sewell,** the Cleveland Indians shortstop, was struck out twice in the same game on May 26, 1930. He finished the season with only one more strikeout, for a total of three.

- **Germany Schaefer,** who played for the Pirates and other National League teams from 1901 to 1918, once reached second base on a double. Then, a few moments later, he stole first. He later said that he had done it to confuse the pitcher.

- **Ty Cobb,** perhaps baseball's greatest player, who set 90 records in his career, went hitless in the three World Series in which he played.

- In 1953, the **St. Louis Browns'** last season before moving to Baltimore, the team had lost 14 games in a row. And they were to face the Yankees, who had won 18 in a row. Manager Marty Marion of the Browns ran into sportswriter Milt Richman in the clubhouse. Marion was so discouraged he handed his empty lineup card to Richman and said, "Here, you make it out." Richman declined, but Marion was insistent. "Pick out any nine you like." Richman did, and the Browns won the game.

- The score of a forfeited ball game is 9–0.

- On July 30, 1937, Phillies first baseman **Dolf Camilli** played the entire game without a putout as Philadelphia beat the Reds 1–0.

- Sixteen-time Golden Glove winner **Brooks Robinson,** third baseman for the Orioles, made three errors in the sixth inning of a game against the A's on July 28, 1971.

○ In 1968, **Tom Tresh,** the Yankees shortstop, played three straight games without having a fielding chance.

○ On August 23, 1952, during a game against the Cardinals, the Giants' **Bob Elliott** complained about a called strike two and kicked dirt on umpire Augie Donatelli. He was ejected, and Bobby Hoffman finished the at bat by being called out on strikes. Hoffman was also ejected for arguing the call.

○ In his only major league appearance on September 29, 1963, **John Paciorek** of the Colt 45s went three for three with three runs batted in and four runs scored against the Mets. A back injury ended his career.

○ In 1950, utility infielder **Pete Castiglione** of the Pirates made ten errors—one at first base, two at second base, three at third base, and four at shortstop.

○ In 1934, the confident Giants manager, **Bill Terry,** when asked about the Dodgers, said, "Brooklyn? Is Brooklyn still in the league?" With two games to go in the season, the Giants were tied with the Cardinals for first place. But the Dodgers beat them in both games, and they lost the pennant. This caused sportswriter John Kieran of the *New York Times* to write a poem:

> Why Mister Terry, oh!, why did you ever
> Chortle the query that made Brooklyn hot?
> Just for the crack that you thought was so clever,
> Now you stand teetering right on the spot!
> Vain was your hope they forgave or forgot;
> Now that you're weary and bowed with fatigue.
> Here is the drama and this is the plot:
> Brooklyn, dear fellow, is still in the league.

O Every major league franchise but the Expos, the Astros, the Mariners, the Angels, the Rangers, and, of course, the Marlins and Rockies, has won at least one **league pennant**. Here then are the pennant winners in order of number of flags won, as of the 1992 season.

Yankees	33	Twins (Senators 3, Min. 3)	6
Dodgers (L.A. 9, Bkn. 9)	18		
Giants (N.Y. 14, S.F. 2)	16	Braves (Bos. 2, Mil. 2, Atl. 2)	6
Cardinals	15		
A's (Phil. 8, Oak. 6)	14	Phillies	4
Cubs	10	White Sox	4
Pirates	9	Indians	3
Red Sox	9	Mets	3
Tigers	9	Royals	2
Reds	9	Brewers	1
Orioles		Padres	1
(ST.L. Browns 1, Bal. 6)	7	Blue Jays	1

O Every franchise in the major leagues except the Expos, the Astros, the Mariners, the Angels, the Rangers, the Brewers, the Padres, and, of course, the Marlins and the Rockies, has won at least one World Series. Here are the teams and the number of series won, in descending order, as of the 1992 season.

Yankees	22	Twins (Wash. 1, Minn. 2)	3
Cardinals	9	Indians	2
A's (Phi. 5, Oak. 3)	8	Mets	2
Pirates	7	White Sox	2
Dodgers (Bkn. 1, L.A. 5)	6	Braves (Bos. 1, Mil. 1)	2
Red Sox	5	Cubs	2
Giants (N.Y. 5)	5	Royals	1
Reds	5	Phillies	1
Tigers	4	Blue Jays	1
Orioles (Bal. 3)	3		

More Baseball Bits

○ The record for number of **World Series games umpired** belongs to Hall of Famer, Bill Klem of the National League—104.

○ Listed below are Twenty-nine **Hall of Famers** who never played major league baseball:

Al Barlick (umpire),
Ed Barrow (executive)
Cool Papa Bell (Negro
  Leagues)
Morgan C. Bulkeley
  (executive)
Alexander Cartwright (in-
  ventor of baseball)
Henry Chadwick
  (sportswriter)
A. B. "Happy" Chandler
  (executive)
Oscar Charleston (Negro
  Leagues)
Thomas H. Connolly
  (umpire)
Ray Dandridge (Negro
  Leagues)
Martin Dehigo (Negro
  Leagues)
Billy Evans (umpire)
Rube Foster (Negro
  Leagues)

Ford Frick (executive)
Josh Gibson (Negro
  Leagues)
Warren Giles (executive)
Will Harridge (executive)
Cal Hubbard (umpire)
Ban Johnson (executive)
Judy Johnson (Negro
  Leagues)
Bill Klem (umpire)
Kenesaw Mountain Landis
  (executive)
Buck Leonard (Negro
  Leagues)
Pop Lloyd (Negro Leagues)
Larry MacPhail (executive)
Bill McGowan (umpire)
Bill Veeck (executive)
George Weiss (executive)
Tom Yawkey (executive)

○ On July 4, 1912, **Ty Cobb** of the Tigers stole second, third, and home in the first inning against the St. Louis Browns.

○ **Cal Hubbard,** the American League umpire who was elected to the Hall of Fame in 1976, was also elected to the Pro Football Hall of Fame (1963) and the National Football Foundation Hall of Fame for college players (1963).

○ **Bill McKechnie** was the only manager to win the World Series with two different National League clubs—the 1925 Pirates and the 1940 Reds.

○ **Bucky Harris** was the only manager to win the World Series with two different American League clubs—the 1924 Senators and the 1947 Yankees.

○ In circling the bases running out his record 755 home runs, **Hank Aaron** trotted a total of 51.5 miles.

○ In running to first base for his record 3,215 singles, **Pete Rose** covered 54.8 miles.

○ **Ty Cobb** of the Tigers set a record by getting five or more hits in 14 different games.

○ On July 13, 1896, **Ed Delahanty,** the Phillies left fielder, hit four home runs—one to left, one to right, one to center, and one inside the park.

○ Catcher **Luke Sewall** of the Senators tagged out two runners at home plate on the same play on April 29, 1933. Lou Gehrig of the Yankees had held up, thinking a fly ball would be caught. The ball fell in for a hit and Gehrig, followed by Dixie Walker right behind him, was tagged out trying to score.

○ **Pete Rose** of the Reds was named to the All-Star Game at five different positions—first base, second base, third base, left field, and right field.

○ The **Chicago Cubs** have won more regular-season games than any other professional team in any sport—8,852 as of the end of the 1992 season.

○ Center fielder **Bob Johnson** drove in all of Philadelphia's runs as the Athletics beat the Browns 8–3 on June 12, 1938.

○ First baseman **Bob Watson** was the first to hit for the cycle in both leagues—with the Astros in 1977 and the Red Sox in 1979.

○ A total of **17 runs** were **scored** in the ninth inning—seven by the Giants and ten by the Braves—on June 20, 1912, as the Giants won the game, 21–12.

○ On April 20, 1988, center fielder **Claudell Washington** hit the 10,000th homer in Yankee history—off the Twins' Jeff Reardon.

○ On June 24, 1962, **Jack Reed,** a utility outfielder for the Yankees, hit a home run in the 22nd inning, for a 9–7 victory over the Tigers. It was the only homer he hit in his three-year career.

○ On June 29, 1986, the Tigers beat the Brewers to give manager **Sparky Anderson** his 600th American League win. He became the first manager to win 600 games in each league, since he had won 863 with the Reds.

○ The **Cubs** and the **Reds** played a nine-inning game with just one baseball on June 29, 1916.

○ On July 11, 1954, third baseman **Jim Commands** of the Phillies hit a grand slam home run against the Dodgers for his first major league hit. In his two-year career, he got only three more hits.

○ Pitcher **Doc Medich** of the Rangers, a medical student in the off-season, saved the life of a 61-year-old fan who suffered a heart attack just before a game in Baltimore on July 17, 1978. Medich administered heart massage until emergency help arrived.

○ The National League home run crown of 1902 was won by Pirate third baseman **Tommy Leach**. He hit a grand total of six four-baggers, and all six of them were inside-the-park jobs.

○ **Hank Aaron** might have had 756 career home runs instead of his record 755. On August 18, 1965, he hit a pitch on top of the pavilion roof at Sportsman's Park in St. Louis, but umpire Chris Pelakoudas called him out for being out of the batter's box when he hit the ball.

○ Early in the twentieth century, manager **Connie Mack** of the Philadelphia Athletics awarded star pitcher Rube Waddell a contract that stated that Waddell's battery mate, Ossee Schreckengost, could not eat crackers in bed when the pair shared a room on the road. In those days, players had to share not only a hotel room when traveling, but the same bed as well.

○ Two Hall of Famers each had their numbers retired by two teams in the same city in different leagues. **Hank Aaron's** number 44 was retired by his first and last teams, the Milwaukee Braves and the Milwaukee Brewers, and **Casey Stengel's** 37 was retired by the New York Yankees and the New York Mets.

○ **Frank Baker,** the slugger for the Athletics and the Yankees, whose nickname was "Home Run" Baker, hit only 94 homers in his 13-year career (1980–1922). That wasn't a bad record because in those days homers were rare.

○ **Rusty Staub** and **Ty Cobb** were the only two players to hit their first home runs as teenagers and their last after they were 40 years old.

○ The player who holds the record for most home runs is **Sadahuru Oh,** of the Yomiuri Giants in Japan, who hit 868 round-trippers in his 21-year career.

○ Hall of Fame hitter **Rogers Hornsby** (1896–1963) guarded his eyesight by not going to the movies. He thought the flickering movement on the screen would hurt his eyes.

○ **Frank Robinson** and **Rusty Staub** share the record for most stadiums in which they hit home runs in regular-season games—32.

○ On August 4, 1982, **Joel Youngblood** got hits for two teams on the same day. He doubled for the Mets in Chicago in an afternoon game. He was then told that he had been traded to the Expos. He flew to Philadelphia, where Montreal was playing a night game, and got a single.

○ In 1957, first baseman **Julio Becquer** of the **Senators** led the team in stolen bases with three. The club had a total of only 13.

○ Not only was **Frank Robinson** the first black man to manage in both the National and American Leagues, he was the first man to be named Most Valuable Player in both leagues, the first to hit 200 or more home runs in both leagues, and the first to hit homers for both leagues in the All-Star Game.

○ On April 22, 1959, the **White Sox** scored 11 runs in one inning while getting only one hit. In the seventh inning they drew ten walks off the A's, and eight of them came with the bases loaded. There were also three errors and a hit batsman, and the Sox still left three men on base in the inning.

○ The one-millionth major league run was scored by first baseman **Bob Watson** of the Astros on May 4, 1975.

○ On August 4, 1919, the **Indians,** with one out to go, scored nine runs in the ninth inning, thus beating the **Yankees** 14–6.

○ In one of the wildest games ever played, the **Cubs** beat the **Phillies,** 26-23 on August 25, 1922. Chicago led 25-6 in the fourth inning but held on as the game ended with the Phillies leaving the bases loaded.

○ On July 17, 1990, the Minnesota Twins set a record by pulling off two triple plays in one game against the Boston Red Sox, but still lost the game, 1–0.

○ Andre Dawson was given a record five intentional walks by opposing pitchers, as the Chicago Cubs beat the Cincinnati Reds, 2–1 on May 22, 1990.

○ Billy Hatcher, the Reds outfielder, set the record for most consecutive World Series hits—seven—in 1990.

○ Hatcher also tied a record of five consecutive extra-base hits in two games of a World Series in 1990. Lou Brock accomplished this in 1968.

○ Don Baylor, who played for 19 years in the American League, set the record for most times being hit by a pitch—225.

○ When Ken Griffey, Jr. won the MVP award in the 1992 All-Star Game, he and his father became the first father-son winners of the award. Ken Griffey, Sr. won it in 1980.

Pitchers

○ On June 7, 1938, Indians pitcher **Johnny Allen** walked off the mound in the second inning after umpire Bill McGowan asked that his dangling sweatshirt sleeve be cut off because it was distracting to Red Sox hitters. Allen was fined $250 by manager Ossie Vitt and the shirt ended up in the Hall of Fame.

○ The three pitchers with the **worst batting averages** were Ron Herbel (Giants, 1963–1971), .029 (six for 206); Andy McGaffigan (Expos, 1981–1988), .040 (five for 124); and Ed Klepfer (Yankees, White Sox, and Indians, 1911–1919), .048 (six for 125).

○ The single-season record of **hitless at-bats in a row** is 70 straight, set by Bob Buhl of the Braves and Cubs in 1962.

○ **Lefty O'Doul** of the Red Sox allowed 13 runs in the first six innings of a game as the Indians won, 27–3. This effectively ended his three-year major league pitching career. But in 1928, he came back as a great-hitting outfielder for the Giants, the Phillies, the Dodgers, and the Giants again.

○ On July 22, 1906, **Bob Ewing** of the Reds beat the Phillies, 10–3, without a single assist being registered by his teammates on the ball club.

○ **Joe "Iron Man" McGinnity** of the Giants won both ends of a doubleheader twice in one week in 1903.

○ **Warren Spahn** of the Braves struck out 18 Cubs in a 15-inning game on June 14, 1952, but lost the game, 3–1.

○ The **St. Louis Browns** used nine pitchers in nine innings against the White Sox on October 2, 1949, as the Sox beat them, 4–3.

○ On April 16, 1940, **Bob Feller** of the Indians beat the White Sox, 1–0, as he pitched a no-hitter—the only opening day no-hitter in major league history.

○ In 1946, when he was 28 years old, Bob Feller's fast ball was clocked at 107.9 miles per hour.

○ When there were only eight teams, pitcher **Warren Spahn** of the Milwaukee Braves hit a home run in every National League park.

○ On September 26, 1908, **Ed Reulbach** of the Cubs became the only pitcher to throw two shutouts in a doubleheader. He beat the Brooklyn Superbas, 5–0 and 3–0, in two nine-inning games.

○ **Dizzy Dean** of the Cardinals was the last National League pitcher to win at least 30 games in one season in 1934 (30–7). In the American League, the feat was last accomplished by Denny McLain of the Tigers in 1968 (31–6). Both wore number 17. In 1934, Dean's Cardinals beat the Tigers in seven games in the World Series. In 1968, McLain's Tigers returned the favor.

○ The highest composite win totals of two pitchers who faced each other were featured on June 9, 1986, when **Tom Seaver** of the White Sox (306 wins) opposed **Don Sutton** of the Angels (298 wins). Sutton won, 3–0.

○ In 1945, **Dick Fowler** of the Athletics threw a no-hitter at the Browns on September 9, winning 1–0. It was the only game he won all year.

○ **Dwight Gooden** of the Mets is the only pitcher to strike out 200 batters in each of his first three years in the major leagues.

○ On September 16, 1981, **Nolan Ryan** of the **Astros** became the first pitcher ever to throw five no-hit, no-run games with a 5–0 victory over the Dodgers at the Astrodome. He now has seven.

○ **Walter Johnson** of the **Senators** pitched his third consecutive shutout in four days on September 7, 1908, with a two-hit victory over the New York Highlanders. He might have done it in three days, but Washington had had a day off on Sunday, September 6.

○ On May 26, 1959, **Harvey Haddix** of the Pirates pitched 12 hitless innings before losing to the Braves, 1–0, in the 13th inning on an error, a sacrifice hit, and Joe Adcock's double.

○ Cincinnati pitchers **Johnny Klippstein, Hersh Freeman,** and **Joe Black** combined for 9⅓ hitless innings on May 26, 1956, but the Reds still lost an 11-inning decision to the Phillies, 2–1.

○ On May 13, 1942, Braves pitcher **Jim Tobin** hit three straight home runs as Boston beat the Cubs, 6–5.

○ **Bob Feller,** the Indians future Hall of Fame pitcher, struck out 15 batters in his first appearance in the major leagues in 1936. In his second game, he tied the record by striking out 17 Athletics on September 13. After those two games, he returned home to Van Meter, Iowa, to finish high school. He had signed with the Indians for a bonus of a one-dollar bill and an autographed baseball. When he returned in 1938, he set a record with 18 strikeouts in a single game.

○ Hall of Fame pitcher **Early Wynn** had won 299 games so far in his career and wanted to get his 300th. He was allowed to go with the White Sox to spring training in 1963, but could not make the team. His old team, the Indians, took him on, and in his fifth start, he won number 300.

○ The **best relief job** in baseball history was probably the performance by Ernie Shore of the Red Sox on June 23, 1917. The Sox starting pitcher walked the first batter, then got in an argument with the umpire and was taken out of the game. Shore relieved and pitched a perfect game—no hits and no walks—and the batter who had walked was thrown out trying to steal second base. The starting pitcher had been Babe Ruth.

○ Browns pitcher **Harry Kimberlin** won his first game in 1939—but it was during his fourth year with the club.

○ Perhaps the **toughest no-hit, no-run game ever pitched** was thrown by Sam Jones of the Cubs on May 12, 1955. In the ninth inning, he walked the bases full and then struck out the next three Pirate batters to win, 4–0.

○ The 1968 **Indians** had the only pitching staff ever to finish the season with more strikeouts than runs allowed. Among the pitchers were Luis Tiant, Steve Hargan, Sam McDowell, Sonny Siebert, and Stan Williams.

Money Matters

○ Hall of Famer **Ralph Kiner** led the National League in home runs in 1952 with 37, but Pirates General Manager Branch Rickey

pointed out that the team had finished in last place, which they could have done without Kiner. So the left fielder took a pay cut.

○ First baseman **Jimmie Foxx** of the Philadelphia Athletics hit 48 home runs, scored 125 runs, and batted in 163 runs with a batting average of .356 in 1933. He was also voted in as Most Valuable Player in the American League. But Athletics manager and owner Connie Mack cut his salary from $16,333 to $16,000. Mack was notoriously tight with a dollar.

○ The **first umpires** in the National League were paid five dollars a day.

○ In 1900, the National League established a **player salary** limitation of $2,400 per year.

○ In 1933, the **Boston Braves** earned a modest $5,000 from the radio broadcasts of their games. In 1936, the **Giants** sold their radio broadcasting rights for $100,000.

○ The **1947 World Series** was the first to be televised, and the rights were sold for $65,000.

○ In 1988, major league teams bought **baseballs** that cost about $38 a dozen.

○ The **average pay** to major league baseball players in 1988 was $433,000.

○ The **Cubs,** who installed lights in Wrigley Field in 1988, paid less than $600 per night game to illuminate the field.

○ In a 1992 survey, it was calculated that the average family of four spends $85.85 to go to a baseball game. That was an increase of 10 percent over 1991. The cheapest costs were at Riverfront Stadium in Cincinnati ($72.28), and the most expensive were at Skydome in Toronto ($112.83 American dollars). These figures included the prices of four seats, two beers, four hot dogs, four soft drinks, two souvenir caps, two programs, and parking.

Miscellaneous Trivia

○ The All-Star pitcher **Sandy Koufax** had a clause in his contract that he would not pitch on the Jewish High Holy Days. So in the first game of the 1965 World Series on October 6, the Dodger star, who had gone 26–8, did not throw against the Twins because it was Yom Kippur.

○ Hall of Fame executive **Branch Rickey,** a devout Christian, did not play on Sundays while he was a major league catcher (1905–1907, 1914).

○ The **National League** goes through about 4,000 dozen baseballs per year.

○ **Wilbert "Uncle Robbie" Robinson,** while the manager of the Dodgers in the 1920s, tried to keep his players on their toes by forming a "Bonehead Club." A Dodger who pulled a "bonehead" play was obliged to pay a fine to the club. The first member was Robinson himself, who walked up to home plate prior to a game and handed the umpire the wrong lineup card.

○ On September 15, 1946, the **Dodgers** beat the **Cubs** 2–0 in five innings. The game was called because of gnats, who became a problem for the players, umpires, and fans.

○ Probably the most even game ever played was between the **Brooklyn Superbas** and the **Pirates** on August 13, 1910. They played to an 8–8 tie, with each team getting 38 at-bats, 13 hits, 12 assists, two errors, five strikeouts, three walks, one hit batsman, and one passed ball.

○ Hall of Fame outfielder **Edd Roush** used a 48-ounce bat—the heaviest ever in the major leagues.

○ First baseman **Ted Kluszewski** of the Reds had such muscular arms that he had to cut the sleeves of his uniform to get into it.

○ **Bert Campaneris** of the Kansas City A's played all nine positions in a single game on September 8, 1965.

○ **Babe Ruth** named his bat "Black Beauty."

○ **"Wee Willie" Keeler,** at five feet and one-half inch tall and 142 pounds, is the smallest player in the Hall of Fame.

○ On August 2, 1938, the **Dodgers** and the **Cardinals** used a yellow baseball as an experiment in the first game of a double header. The Dodgers won the game, 6–2, and the yellow ball was never used again.

○ When **Comiskey Park** was built in Chicago in 1910, the owner of the White Sox modestly called it "Charles A. Comiskey's Baseball Palace."

○ On June 26, 1944, in an effort to raise funds for World War II war bonds, the **Giants, Dodgers,** and **Yankees** played against each other in a six-inning game at the Polo Grounds in New York. More than 50,000 fans turned out as each team played successive innings against the other two teams, then sat out an inning. The final score was Dodgers-5, Yankees-1, Giants-0.

○ During **World War II,** American soldiers in their foxholes taunted their Japanese adversaries with nasty references to Emperor Hirohito. The Japanese frequently replied with what they considered the only fitting retort: "To hell with Babe Ruth."

○ The Hall of Fame received a letter from the *Sporting News* in 1985 addressed to **Abner Doubleday,** (1819–1893) the alleged originator of baseball. The letter informed Doubleday that his subscription had been cancelled.

○ When the seventh edition of *The Baseball Encyclopedia* was published in 1988, **Lou Proctor,** listed in previous editions as a member of the 1912 Browns, was missing. It was discovered that Proctor was actually a press-box telephone operator who decided to enter his name in the box score. He remained a "Player" with a one-game career until researchers weeded him out. All those years he was listed as having no hits, no at-bats, and one walk.

○ **Marge Schott**, the owner of the Reds, required her scouts to make calls from pay phones rather than from their rooms to avoid hotel surcharges. In 1988, she went to Rome and took a gift for the Pope—a Reds warmup jacket with John Paul II inscribed on the back.

○ In an exhibition game in Raleigh, North Carolina, **Wake Forest** and **North Carolina State** played a nine-inning baseball game with a mechanical pitcher. Each team stationed a man near the machine to do the fielding. Wake Forest won, 8–0, getting 11 hits to three. The robot was charged with seven walks and one wild pitch.

○ **Charles O. Finley**, when he owned the Oakland A's, bought a mascot—a mule named Charlie O.

○ On February 4, 1962, in a supplement to the Soviet newspaper, *Izvestia,* "beisbol" was reported to be an old Russian game.

○ When the pitcher, catcher, and umpire get into an argument, baseball announcers call it "a rhubarb." The word comes from a sound effects technique used in early radio dramas. Whenever a director wanted the sound of an angry, menacing crowd, he would have five or six actors mutter "rhubarb-rhubarb-rhubarb" over and over, which recreated the effective simulation of a large and belligerent mob. Ever since, the word "rhubarb" has meant a loud and heated dispute.

○ In 1988, **Art Ditmar,** the former Yankee pitcher, lost his lawsuit against a beer company and an advertising agency that had mistakenly identified him as the pitcher who had given up Pirate Bill Mazeroski's home run that won the 1960 World Series.

Actually, it was Ralph Terry, but the judge ruled that Ditmar failed to provide more than speculation that the commercial had caused him any financial harm, such as playing in old-timers games and golf tournaments.

○ In 1987, the Cardinals, the National League pennant winners, had so many injuries that they voted **Dr. Stan London,** their team doctor, a half-share in their World Series winnings. It amounted to $28,026.26.

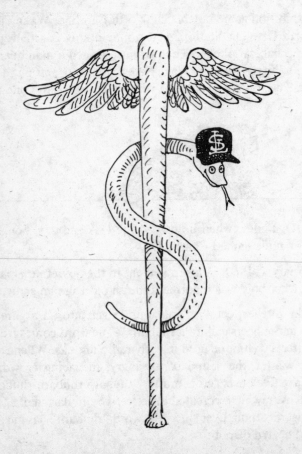

○ On July 11, 1990, during the last year of their old Comiskey Park, the Chicago White Six played a baseball nostalgia game. They wore uniforms like their 1917 world champion forerunners and used a hand-operated scoreboard. Popcorn cost five cents, and general admission tickets went for 50 cents. But the Milwaukee Brewers won the game, 12–9, in 13 innings.

○ On September 23, 1990, American League umpire Ken Kaiser's luggage was lost by an airline on its way to Kansas City. Kaiser umpired at second base dressed in a sweatsuit with "Royals" on the shirt and pant legs as Kansas City beat Oakland, 10–3.

○ With the Republican National Convention being held in Houston in August, 1992, in the Astrodome, the Astros had no place to play their home games. They were forced to go on a 28-game road trip that lasted from July 27 to August 23.

○ As of August, 1992, the Houston Astros were fielding the youngest team in the National League, and the Cleveland Indians were the youngest in the American League. The average age of major league teams was as follows:

NATIONAL LEAGUE		AMERICAN LEAGUE	
Astros	27.12	Indians	26.76
Phillies	27.96	Mariners	28.29
Braves	28.35	Orioles	28.57
Cubs	28.36	Royals	28.59
Expos	28.46	Twins	28.75
Reds	28.66	Angels	29.11
Cardinals	28.92	Brewers	29.19
Giants	28.97	Rangers	29.30
Padres	29.36	White Sox	29.58
Pirates	29.65	Yankees	29.70
Mets	30.04	Blue Jays	29.99
Dodgers	30.46	Tigers	30.44
		Red Sox	30.65
		A's	31.74

What's in a Name?

One of the best things about baseball has been—and always will be—the players' names and nicknames. Only in baseball will you find a pitcher named Rollie Fingers, a shortstop called "Scooter" (Phil Rizzuto), or a slugger called the "Sultan of Swat" (Babe Ruth). Below are some of the best names in baseball.

He's Not Who You Think He Is

Because of the sheer number of players in major league baseball, it's no surprise that some of them would have the same names as famous personalities. Here are some of the better ones and the teams they were most closely associated with.

HE'S NOT THE PRESIDENT

John Adams, Phillies catcher
James Buchanan, Browns pitcher
John Kennedy, Red Sox third baseman
John Tyler, Boston Braves pitcher
George Washington, White Sox pitcher

HE'S NOT THE SENATOR, CONGRESSMAN, OR GOVERNOR

Howard Baker, Cleveland Molly McGuires third baseman
Bill Bradley, Cleveland Bronchos third baseman
John Calhoun, Cardinals third baseman
John Glenn, Cardinals outfielder
Robert Kennedy, White Sox outfielder
Ted Kennedy, Cubs pitcher
Tip O'Neill, Reds outfielder
Al Smith, White Sox outfielder

HE'S NOT THE TRAILBLAZER OR SCOUT FROM U.S. HISTORY

Daniel Boone, Padres pitcher
Kit Carson, Indians outfielder
Davey Crockett, Tigers first baseman

HE'S NOT THE GENERAL

Ethan Allen, Reds outfielder
George Patton, Philadelphia Athletics

HE'S NOT THE WRITER

Robert Burns, White Sox pitcher
Ben Johnson, Cubs pitcher
Earl Wilson, Red Sox pitcher

HE'S NOT THE MUSICIAN

James Brown, Cardinals outfielder
James Brown, Rangers pitcher
Phil Collins, Phillies pitcher
Eddie Fisher, White Sox pitcher
Tom Jones, Cardinals first baseman
Rickey Nelson, Mariners outfielder
Johnny Ray, Pirates second baseman

HE'S NOT THE PERFORMER

Jack Barry, Philadelphia Athletics shortstop
Ed Begley, New York Giants pitcher
Ken Berry, White Sox outfielder
John Davidson, Twins outfielder
Robert Reed, Tigers pitcher
Mike Wallace, Cardinals pitcher

HE'S NOT THE MOVIE STAR

Matthew Broderick, Brooklyn Superbas second baseman
Gary Cooper, Atlanta Braves outfielder
William Powell, Pirates pitcher
John Houseman, Cardinals second baseman
George C. Scott, Red Sox first baseman
Robert Shaw, San Francisco Giants pitcher
Jimmy Stewart, Cubs outfielder
Robert Taylor, San Francisco Giants outfielder

HE'S NOT THE COMEDIAN

George Burns, Indians first baseman
George Burns, New York Giants outfielder
Eddie Murphy, White Sox outfielder
Bill Murray, Senators second baseman
Danny Thomas, Brewers outfielder

HE'S NOT THE AUTO RACING CHAMPION

Johnny Rutherford, Brooklyn Dodgers pitcher
Al Unser, Tigers catcher

HE'S NOT THE BASKETBALL STAR

Bill Russell, Los Angeles Dodgers shortstop

HE'S NOT THE BOXER

Joe Frazier, Cardinals outfielder
Archie Moore, Yankees outfielder
John L. Sullivan, Boston Braves outfielder
Mike Tyson, Cardinals second baseman

HE'S NOT THE MOTEL FOUNDER

Howard Johnson, Mets third baseman

HE'S NOT THE TEAM OWNER

Ted Turner, Cubs pitcher

Neat Nicknames

Baseball players have always had interesting nicknames. There have been clever ones, such as the nickname given to Doug Gwosdz, the Padres catcher, who was called "Eyechart," and disgusting ones, such as the nickname given to Nick Cullop, the Reds outfielder, "Tomato Face." Even those players who seemed to have enough names to begin with were often given an extra one or two. Take Christian Frederick Albert John Henry David Betzel, the Cardinals second baseman, who was called "Bruno"; Indians pitcher Calvin Coolidge Julius Caesar Tuskahoma McLish, called "Cal" and "Buster"; and Alan Mitchell Edward George Patrick Henry Gallagher, the Giants third baseman, who was called "Dirty Al." Below are some of the more amusing nicknames in baseball. The teams listed and positions played are the ones with whom the players are most commonly associated.

WOMEN'S NAMES

"Beverly" Bayne, Browns pitcher

"Tilly" Bishop, Philadelphia Athletics second baseman

"Lu" Blue, Tigers first baseman

"Kitty" Bransfield, Phillies first baseman

"Mary" Calhoun, Boston Braves first baseman

"Rosy" Carlisle, Red Sox outfielder

"Molly" Craft, Senators pitcher

"Dolly" Gray, Pirates first baseman

"Bubbles" Hargrave, Reds catcher

"Zaza" Harvey, Indians outfielder

"Bonnie" Hollingsworth, Senators pitcher

"Sadie" Houck, Boston Braves outfielder

"Little Eva" Lange, Cubs outfielder

"Polly" McLarry, Cubs first baseman

"Molly" Meloan, White Sox outfielder

"Minny" Mendoza, Twins third baseman

"Mollie" Milosevich, Yankees shortstop

"Molly" Molinaro, Tigers outfielder

"Ivy" Olson, Brooklyn shortstop

"Rosy" Ryan, New York Giants pitcher

"Tillie" Shafer, New York Giants third baseman

"Dolly" Stark, Brooklyn shortstop

"Lil" Stoner, Tigers pitcher

"Tilly" Walker, Phillies outfielder

FOOD NAMES

"Liver" Ancker, Philadelphia Athletics pitcher

"Sweetbreads" Bailey, Cubs pitcher

"Chops" Broskie, Boston Braves catcher

"Soup" Campbell, Indians outfielder

"Doughnut Bill" Carrick, New York Giants pitcher

"Cookie" Cuccurullo, Pirates pitcher

"Chili" Davis, San Francisco Giants outfielder

"Pickles" Dillhoefer, Cardinals catcher

"Pea Soup" Dumont, Senators pitcher

"Pickles" Gerken, Indians outfielder
"T-Bone" Giordano, Philadelphia Athletics second baseman
"Noodles" Hahn, Reds pitcher
"Cracker" Hamby, New York Giants catcher
"Hot Potato" Hamlin, Brooklyn pitcher
"Pork Chop" Hoffman, Astros catcher
"Tomatoes" Kafora, Pirates catcher
"Beans" Keener, Phillies pitcher
"T-Bone" Koski, Pirates pitcher
"Peanuts" Lowery, Cubs outfielder
"Spinach" Melillo, Browns second baseman
"Peach Pie" O'Connor, Cardinals catcher
"Little Potato" Pascual, Twins pitcher
"Ham" Patterson, Browns first baseman
"Pretzels" Pezzullo, Phillies pitcher
"Soup" Polivka, Reds pitcher
"Cookie" Rojas, Rangers second baseman
"Ham" Schulte, Phillies second baseman
"Cheese" Schweitzer, Browns outfielder
"Pie" Traynor, Pirates third baseman
"Goober" Zuber, Yankees pitcher
"Noodles" Zupo, Orioles outfielder

Baseball in the Media

Baseball has never been the hottest subject in films or on TV. In the movies, it has always taken a back seat to boxing and thoroughbred racing, and it's never been a very popular subject for TV series. But there are many enjoyable movies, as well as books, songs, and a few poems, on the subject of baseball. Here are some of them.

At the Movies

EARLY FILMS

○ Probably the first baseball movie ever made was a short—*Casey at the Bat*—based on the classic poem about the star of the Mudville Nine. And, believe it or not, it was made by the great inventor, Thomas A. Edison.

○ There are only a few movies from the silent film era worth mentioning and not necessarily because they were good:

Somewhere in Georgia (1916) starred the great Tigers outfielder, Ty Cobb, and is said to be the worst baseball film ever made. In it, Cobb was attacked by bad guys and tied up. He made his escape just in time to race to the ball park on a mule and save the old ball game for the home team.

Even Babe Ruth had a modest movie career. First came *Headin' Home* (1920), followed by *The Babe Comes Home* (1922). For the latter picture he was paid an astronomical (especially in those days) $25,000 for a mere 17 days of shooting. He also had a cameo role in Harold Lloyd's *Speedy,* a 1928 comedy, and as himself in *The Pride of the Yankees* (1942), the biographical picture about his old Yankees teammate, Lou Gehrig.

BIOPICS

○ *The Babe* (1992). John Goodman, Kelly McGillis, Bruce Boxleitner. Goodman plays Babe Ruth in this picture about the man whose appetites were as gigantic as his talent. But the critics, although admitting it was better than *The Babe Ruth Story*, scored it as a double rather than a home run.

○ *The Babe Ruth Story* (1948). William Bendix, Claire Trevor, Charles Bickford. Bendix stars as the Bambino in this sentimental, inaccurate biography.

○ *Don't Look Back: The Story of Leroy "Satchel" Paige* (1981). Louis Gossett, Jr., Cleavon Little, Ossie Davis. This is the biography of the legendary pitcher, based on his own book, *Maybe I'll Pitch Forever.*

○ *Fear Strikes Out* (1957). Anthony Perkins, Karl Malden, Norma Moore. Perkins brilliantly plays the fine Red Sox outfielder, Jimmy Piersall, whose career was affected by a mental breakdown. Malden plays his ambitious father.

○ *It's Good to Be Alive* (TV movie, 1974). Paul Winfield, Louis Gossett, Jr., Ruby Dee. This is the story of Roy Campanella, the Hall of Fame Dodgers catcher, who was crippled in an automobile accident.

○ *The Jackie Robinson Story* (1950). Jackie Robinson, Ruby Dee. Robinson plays himself in this biopic that tells of the early years of the first black man in major league baseball.

○ *The Pride of St. Louis* (1952). Dan Dailey, Joanne Dru, Richard Crenna. The biography of Dizzy Dean, the famed Cardinals pitcher. Dailey does a fine job as Dean.

○ *The Pride of the Yankees* (1942). Gary Cooper, Theresa Wright, Babe Ruth, Walter Brennan, Dan Duryea. Cooper plays the legendary Lou Gehrig, the Yankees' first baseman. Although Cooper was a natural right-hander, he wore a mirror-image uniform and seemed to be left-handed when the film was reversed, and his acting was first-rate.

○ *The Stratton Story* (1949). James Stewart, June Allyson, Frank Morgan, Bill Williams. This is the biopic of the outstanding White Sox pitcher, Monty Stratton, who made a successful minor league comeback after losing his leg in a hunting accident. Screenwriter Douglas Morrow won an Oscar for the best original story.

○ *The Winning Team* (1952). Ronald Reagan, Doris Day, Frank Lovejoy. Reagan plays Grover Cleveland Alexander, the Hall of Fame pitcher for the Phillies and Cubs, who died in poverty.

MOVIE MUSICALS

○ *Damn Yankees* (1958). Gwen Verdon, Tab Hunter, Ray Walston. This musical features a diehard, middle-aged Washington Senator fan who sells his soul to the Devil. The Devil transforms him into a youthful superstar who leads the Senators to the pennant over the hated Yankees.

○ *Take Me Out to the Ball Game* (1948). Frank Sinatra, Esther Williams, Gene Kelly, Betty Garrett, Jules Munshin. A fun musical about the early days of baseball in which Williams owns a ball club with a versatile double-play combination ("O'Brien to Ryan to Goldberg").

COMEDIES, DRAMAS, AND FANTASIES

○ *Angels in the Outfield* (1951). Paul Douglas, Janet Leigh, Keenan Wynn. This fantasy about the Pittsburgh Pirates features an orphan who sees angels that give advice about how to win baseball games.

○ *The Bad News Bears* (1976). Walter Matthau, Tatum O'Neal, Vic Morrow, Joyce Van Patten, Brandon Cruz, Jackie Earle Haley. Morris Buttermaker (Matthau) is a former minor league player who cleans swimming pools and signs on to coach a losing Little League team. He recruits the best pitcher he can, an 11-year-old girl (O'Neal). There were also two sequels—both of them pretty bad.

girl (O'Neal). There were also two sequels—both of them pretty bad.

○ *The Bingo Long Traveling All-Stars and Motor Kings* (1976). Billy Dee Williams, James Earl Jones, Richard Pryor. A barnstorming black baseball team of the 1930s tries to outdo the the National Negro League teams in this heartwarming comedy.

○ *Blue Skies Again* (1983). Mimi Rogers, Harry Hamlin, Robyn Barto, Kenneth McMillan. A young woman (Rogers) wants to play professional baseball, and is given a trial.

○ *Bull Durham* (1988). Kevin Costner, Susan Sarandon, Tim Robbins. Life in the minors is accurately depicted in this film about a love triangle between the three main characters.

○ *Eight Men Out* (1988). John Cusack, Clifton James, Christopher Lloyd, David Strathairn, D.B. Sweeney, Charlie Sheen. This film explores the motivations of the eight men involved in the infamous 1919 "Black Sox Scandal."

○ *Field of Dreams* (1989). Kevin Costner, Amy Madigan, James Earl Jones, Burt Lancaster. Costner is believable as an Iowa farmer who has a vision that if he builds a baseball diamond, Shoeless Joe Jackson and other deceased great players will reappear to play there.

○ *It Happens Every Spring* (1949). Ray Milland, Jean Peters, Paul Douglas. Milland is a chemistry professor who discovers a compound which makes baseballs avoid wood, and becomes a star pitcher who can strike out any batter holding a wooden bat.

○ *A League of Their Own* (1992). Geena Davis, Tom Hanks, Madonna. This warm, funny, and sentimental film tells the story of the rocky first season of the Rockford Peaches in the All–American Girls Professional Baseball League. It is the fictional account of a real team in a real league.

○ *Major League* (1989). Tom Berenger, Charlie Sheen, Corbin Bernsen, Bob Uecker. A loveable band of misfits and loonies turn around the fate of the hapless Cleveland Indians.

○ *Mr. Baseball* (1992). Tom Selleck, Ken Takakura. A comedy about an American baseball player who learns about playing in Japan.

○ *The Natural* (1984). Robert Redford, Robert Duvall, Glenn Close, Richard Farnsworth, Kim Basinger, Wilford Brimley, Barbara Hershey. Roy Hobbs (Redford), an all-American hero, strives for perfection as a baseball player, but he is shot with a silver bullet by a young woman, only to make a comeback 15 years later.

○ *Rhubarb* (1951). Ray Milland, Jan Sterling, Gene Lockhart. A millionaire who owns a baseball team dies and wills the team to his cat, Rhubarb, who becomes the mascot and inspires the team to a pennant.

○ *Safe at Home!* (1962). Mickey Mantle, Roger Maris, Don Collier, Bryan Russell, William Frawley. This is a story about a Little Leaguer who runs away from home to the Yankees' training camp to try to get Mantle and Maris to come to his team's banquet.

○ *The Slugger's Wife* (1985). Michael O'Keefe, Rebecca DeMornay, Martin Ritt, Randy Quaid. The story of a rude, boorish baseball player who falls in love with a singer.

○ *Stealing Home* (1988). Jodie Foster, Mark Harmon, Blair Brown. This movie tells of the long-time romance between a girl and a baseball player, and her eventual suicide.

Baseball on TV

For some reason, there have been very few television series that have featured baseball. "Cheers," in which Ted Danson plays a former Red Sox pitcher, and "Who's the Boss?" where Tony Danza plays a former Cardinal, don't really count since those shows are not about baseball.

Baseball sitcoms, never lasted long. "The Bad News Bears" appeared from 1979 to 1980, and "Ball Four" (1976) and "The Bay City Blues" (1983) collapsed after running for less than a full season.

Baseball Books

BOOKS FOR KIDS

○ Leonard Everett Fisher wrote a wonderful science fiction novel about baseball in the future. *Noonan* tells the story of a young man who plays for the Chicago Cubs in the 21st century, when people watch the games on three-dimensional television, instead of at the ball park.

○ *Last Sunday* by Robert Newton Peck is about sandlot baseball in the 1930s. It tells of a girl and her dreams of baseball.

OTHER BASEBALL STORIES

○ *The Natural,* by Bernard Malamud, was later made into a movie starring Robert Redford. It tells of the rise and fall of a talented baseball player.

○ *The Year the Yankees Lost the Pennant,* by Douglas Wallop, is a funny book about a middle-aged Washington Senators baseball fan who sells his soul to the Devil to become a young Senator superstar, and who finally leads his team to the pennant—breaking the Yankee dynasty. The musical comedy *Damn Yankees* was based on this book.

○ Author George Plimpton wrote *The Curious Case of Sidd Finch* as an April Fool joke on the American public. Trained in the Himalayas in the ways of Zen, an English orphan shocks the major leagues with his ability to throw a baseball 168 miles per hour.

○ One of the greatest of American humorists, Ring Lardner, scored his first success in *You Know Me, Al,* a novel about an illiterate and selfish, but extremely talented baseball player.

○ One of the most moving of all baseball stories was written by Mark Harris. His *Bang the Drum Slowly* is about the friendship between an intelligent star baseball pitcher and a dull-witted, second-rate catcher who is suffering from a fatal disease. It was made into a movie starring Robert De Niro and Michael Moriarty.

NONFICTION

○ The first, and still the best, of the baseball expose autobiographies is *Ball Four,* by former pitcher Jim Bouton. It provides new insights into the baseball life off the field, and is very funny at the same time.

○ Arguably the best sports interviewer in the baseball business is Roger Angell. In *The Boys of Summer* and *Season Ticket,* he shows his ability to talk to the players and to get them to give him their innermost thoughts, poignant memories, fears, and humorous stories.

Poetic Musings

"PRAY FOR RAIN"

One of the worst pieces of doggerel was the poem created about the 1948 Boston Braves. They had a pretty mediocre pitching staff, with the exception of Warren Spahn and Johnny Sain, and the poem was "Spahn and Sain and pray for rain." The Braves managed to win the National League pennant that year.

POETRY IN SONG

Songs can qualify as poetry, too, and the most famous of all is "Take Me Out to the Ball Game." It was first heard in 1908, and had words by Jack Norworth and music by Harry von Tilzer. At the time they wrote it, neither one had ever seen a baseball game.

TINKER TO EVERS TO CHANCE

Franklin Pierce Adams, a transplanted Chicagoan, was a columnist for the *New York Daily Mail*. On a July day in 1910, because he needed eight lines to fill out his column, he wrote a poem called "Baseball's Sad Lexicon," which turned a no-better-than-capable Cubs' double-play combination by players Joe Tinker, Johnny Evers, and Frank Chance into a legend:

> These are the saddest of possible words
>> Tinker to Evers to Chance.
> Trio of Bear Cubs and fleeter than birds
>> Tinker to Evers to Chance
> Thoughtlessly pricking our gonfalon bubble,
> Making a Giant hit into a double,
> Words that are weighty with nothing but trouble
>> Tinkers to Evers to Chance.

This bit of doggerel may have made the reputations of all three players and helped them into the Hall of Fame

THE MIGHTY CASEY

The most famous poem of all—a poem that has been beloved for more than 100 years—is *Casey at the Bat*. It was written by Ernest Lawrence Thayer, a Harvard graduate and a close friend of William Randolph Hearst, who became editor of the *San Francisco Examiner,* and who hired Thayer to write a humor column for the paper. His final piece was written in May of 1888, and Thayer said it took only two hours to write. It appeared on Sunday, June 3rd of that year, and he was paid five dollars.

The piece was titled "Casey," and it made little stir at first. But that summer in New York, a tall, handsome 30-year-old singer and comedian named William DeWolf Hopper was appearing at Wallach's Theater. He was a fan of the New York Giants, and decided to stage a "Baseball Night" at the theater. Two days before the scheduled night, a friend shared the poem with him. Hopper presented the poem at the festivities, and the *New York Times* reported that "a thrilling ode entitled 'Casey's at the Bat' was most uproariously received." The poem, now called *Casey at the Bat,* became Hopper's trademark.

In 1895, Thayer sheepishly admitted that he was the author, and later said, "For this, perhaps my greatest of sins, I am exclusively to blame." Mudville, it was said, was really Boston.

CASEY AT THE BAT

The outlook wasn't brilliant for the Mudville nine that day;
The score stood four to two with but one inning more to play.
And then when Cooney died at first, and Barrows did the same,
A sickly silence fell upon the patrons of the game.

A straggling few got up to go in deep despair. The rest
Clung to that hope which springs eternal in the human breast;
They thought if only Casey could but get a whack at that—
We'd put up even money now with Casey at the bat.

But Flynn preceded Casey, as did Jimmy Blake,
And the former was a lulu and the latter was a cake;
So upon that stricken multitude grim melancholy sat,
For there seemed but little chance of Casey's getting to the bat.

But Flynn let drive a single, to the wonderment of all,
And Blake, the much despis-ed, tore the cover off the ball;
And when the dust had lifted, and the men saw what had occurred,
There was Jimmy safe at second and Flynn a-hugging third.

Then from 5,000 throats and more there rose a lusty yell;
It rumbled through the valley, it rattled in the dell;
It knocked upon the mountain and recoiled upon the flat,
For Casey, mighty Casey, was advancing to the bat.

There was ease in Casey's manner as he stepped into his place;
There was pride in Casey's bearing and a smile on Casey's face.
And when, responding to the cheers, he lightly doffed his hat,
No stranger in the crowd could doubt 'twas Casey at the bat.

Ten thousand eyes were on him as he rubbed his hands with dirt;
Five thousand tongues applauded when he wiped them on his shirt.
Then while the writhing pitcher ground the ball into his hip,
Defiance gleamed in Casey's eye, a sneer curled Casey's lip.

And now the leather-covered sphere came hurtling through the air,
And Casey stood a-watching it in haughty grandeur there.
Close by the sturdy batsman the ball unheeded sped—
"That ain't my style," said Casey. "Strike one," the umpire said.

From the benches, black with people, there went up a muffled roar,
Like the beating of the storm-waves on a stern and distant shore.
"Kill him! Kill the umpire!" shouted someone on the stand;
And it's likely they'd have killed him had not Casey raised his hand.

With a smile of Christian charity great Casey's visage shone;
He stilled the rising tumult; he bade the game go on;
He signaled to the pitcher, and once more the spheroid flew;
But Casey still ignored it, and the umpire said, "Strike two."

"Fraud!" cried the maddened thousands, and the echo answered
     fraud;
But one scornful look from Casey and the audience was awed.
They saw his face grow stern and cold, they saw his muscles strain,
And they knew that Casey wouldn't let that ball go by again.

The sneer is gone from Casey's lip, his teeth are clenched in hate;
He pounds with cruel violence his bat upon the plate.
And now the pitcher holds the ball, and now he lets it go,
And now the air is shattered by the force of Casey's blow.

Oh, somewhere in this favored land the sun is shining bright;
The band is playing somewhere, and somewhere hearts are light,
And somewhere men are laughing, and somewhere children shout;
But there is no joy in Mudville—mighty Casey has struck out.

Arts and Letters

That same poem, "Casey at the Bat," keeps popping up, even on the higher artistic level of opera and dance.

In 1953, the American composer, William Schuman, premiered his one-act opera, *The Mighty Casey*, which contained, as the libretto, the Thayer poem. It is still performed occasionally, but usually by college music schools.

The world premiere of a ballet, also called *The Mighty Casey*, was presented in Pittsburgh on October 6, 1990. Danced by the Pittsburgh Ballet Theatre, the choreographer was Lisa de Ribère. It was good enough to cause one critic to rave, "[it is] the first choreographic attempt to combine the moves of the game with the steps of the art for an entire ballet, and it does so with enough style, wit, and accuracy to satisfy fans of both ballpark and theater."

Colleges have even got into the act of making baseball intellectually acceptable. For example, in 1990, The New School for Social Research in New York offered two new courses. "The History of Baseball in America" reviewed the sport from 1839 to the present using a timeline of American history as a scorecard. "The Mystique of Baseball" examined the karma and mythology of the game.

Odds and Ends

The Last Legal Spitball

The last legal spitball was thrown by Hall of Fame member Burleigh "Ol' Stubblebeard" Grimes, a right-handed pitcher for the Yankees, in 1934. That might not seem too important, but the spitball had been declared illegal in 1920.

Grimes began his career with the Pirates in 1916 and moved to the Brooklyn Dodgers in 1918. He continued to play for the Dodgers until 1926. He then pitched for the New York Giants (1927), the Pirates again (1928–1929), the Boston Braves (1930), the Cardinals (1930–1931), the Cubs (1932–1933), the Cardinals again (1933–1934), the Pirates again (1934), and the Yankees (1934). For those 15 years he used an illegal pitch.

The catch was that when the anti-spitball rule was passed, there were several pitchers who relied on it, and each of the 16 major league teams was permitted to name up to two members of its pitching staff as exemptions for the 1920 season. By the 1921 season, 17 pitchers were granted the right to use the spitball for the rest of their careers.

The nine exempted in the American League, with their 1920 won-lost records, were Stan Covelski (21–14) and Ray Caldwell (20–10) of the Indians; Red Faber (23–13) of the White Sox; Jack Quinn (18–10) of the Yankees; Urban Shocker (20–10) and Allen Sothoron (8–15) of the St. Louis Browns; Allen Russell (5–6) of the Red Sox; and Doc Ayers (7–14) and Dutch Leonard (10–17) of the Tigers. In the National League there were eight: Grimes (23–11) and Clarence Mitchell (5–2) of the Dodgers; Phil Douglas (14–10) of the New York Giants; Ray Fisher (10–11) of the Reds; Bill Doak (10–12) and Marv Goodwin (3–8) of the Cardinals; and Dana Fillingim (12–21) and Dick Rudolph (4–8) of the Boston Braves.

Grimes outlasted them all, and ended his career with 270 wins.

The Chicago Black Sox

In 1919, the Chicago White Sox, who had won the American League pennant in 1917, won the pennant easily under manager Kid Gleason. But no one knew that three of the Sox had approached big-time gamblers in New York at mid-season to offer a fix in exchange for a large sum of money. They were pitcher Eddie Cicotte, first baseman Arnold "Chick" Gandil, and pitcher Claude "Lefty" Williams. In the National League, the Reds had won the pennant for the first time, and this created a great deal of Midwest interest in the World Series.

The White Sox were favored, but they lost the series five games to three. It was apparent that many people knew the fix was in, since the odds went from 3–1 White Sox to 8–5 Reds. Supposedly the signal to the gamblers telling them which games were to be thrown was to have the Sox pitcher hit the first batter in game number one. This was done by Cicotte, and the game was won by the Reds, 9–1.

Most people think that after the first game, the series was played more or less honestly, even though Williams did walk three men in one inning in the second game, which was very unusual for him. The Reds won that game, 4–2. The Sox did win the third game, 3–0, but cynics say it was because the gamblers were not paying the players what had been agreed on—$10,000 of the $100,000 total after each game.

Cicotte was on the mound in the fourth game, and lost, 2–0, while making two errors himself. The fifth game was won by the Reds, 5–0, and the sixth was won by the Sox, 5–4. In the seventh game, Cicotte, who had begged to start, actually beat the Reds 4–1. But the final game was all Reds, as they won the game, 10–5, and the series.

The fixing of the series took almost a year to surface. The following September, boxer Abe Attell confessed to being involved in the deal and named eight players as guilty parties. The "Black Sox" on the list were left fielder "Shoeless Joe" Jackson, third baseman George "Buck" Weaver, Gandil, shortstop Charles "Swede" Risberg, Cicotte, Williams, center fielder Oscar "Happy" Felsch, and utility infielder Fred McMullin. The *Chicago Tribune* called for a grand jury investigation.

Cicotte broke down when he was confronted by Manager Gleason and owner Charles Comiskey. He, Jackson, and Williams then confessed to the grand jury, and Comiskey suspended all eight players, although it was argued that Weaver was guilty only by association, since he had sat in on the negotiations and then decided not to participate in the fix. As Jackson was leaving the courthouse, a small boy supposedly came up to him and said, with tears in his eyes, "Say it ain't so, Joe."

Criminal indictments followed, but by then the players' written confessions had disappeared, and they were all acquitted. According to the letter of the law, they all could have been reinstated. But there was a new man in baseball—Commissioner Kenesaw Mountain Landis. He took quick and decisive action. "Regardless of the verdict of juries, no player that throws a game, no player that entertains proposals or promises to throw a game, no player that sits in conference with a bunch of crooks and gamblers where the ways and means of throwing games are discussed, and does not promptly tell his club about it, will ever again play professional baseball."

Some people felt that some of the players deserved a pardon. Weaver never shared in the bribe money and hit .324 in the series.

Ten thousand fans signed a petition calling for his reinstatement. But Landis turned a cold shoulder. Jackson got no fix money and batted .375 in the series, the highest average on either team. But when word got to Landis that Jackson had been hired to coach a Class D minor league team, he ordered him fired.

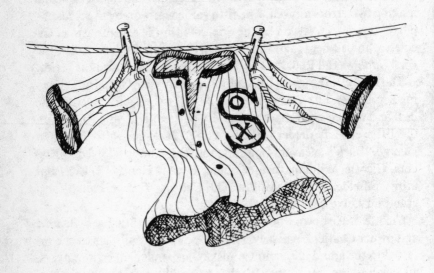

Double-Barrelled Stars

Here are a few fine baseball players who were also stars in other sports.

DANNY AINGE: FROM BATS TO HOOPS

Danny Ainge was an outstanding player in several sports for Brigham Young University. At six feet, four inches tall and 175 pounds, he seemed an ideal player for either baseball or basketball. Ainge tried baseball first as a utility player at second base, third base, shortstop, in the outfield, and even as a designated hitter for the Toronto Blue Jays (1979–1981). But because he was only a .220 hitter and appeared in a mere 211 games in those three years, he decided that basketball was his sport. He went on to become a fast, hustling guard for the Boston Celtics, the Sacramento Kings, the Portland Trail Blazers and the Phoenix Suns, and a deadly free-throw and three-point shooter.

GENE CONLEY: SPLIT PERSONALITY

Gene Conley, a six-foot, eight-inch-tall right-handed pitcher, threw for the Braves in Boston (1952) and in Milwaukee (1954–1958), the Phillies (1959–1960), and the Red Sox (1961–1963). Conley won 91 while losing 96, and carried an earned run average of 3.82. Amazingly, during most of that time he was also a standout professional basketball player, appearing as the center for the Boston Celtics (1950–1960) and the New York Knicks (1961).

LOU GEHRIG: ALL-AROUND ATHLETE

Gehrig, the Hall of Fame Yankee first baseman, was an amazing athlete. At the age of 11 he was able to swim across the Hudson River, and while he was a student at Columbia University, he was a baseball star, and an outstanding football player. He played part of the time as a tackle and part of the time as a halfback. As a lineman, he hit hard on offense and was resourceful on defense. As a triple-threat man, he was a fine blocker but an even better punter.

STEVE HAMILTON: FROM HURLING TO HOOKSHOTS

Steve Hamilton was a left-handed pitcher for the Indians (1961), the Senators (1962–1963), the Yankees (1963–1970), the White Sox (1970), the Giants (1971), and the Cubs (1972). In his 12 years as a pitcher, he won 40 games while losing 31, but saved 42. He also played professional basketball with the Minneapolis Lakers (later the Los Angeles Lakers). He then went on to become the baseball coach and later the athletic director at Morehead State University in Kentucky.

BO JACKSON: DOUBLE DRAFT PICK

Bo Jackson was an outstanding running back for Auburn University, winning the Heisman Trophy in 1985. Drafted by the Royals in baseball and the Raiders in football, he astonished the sports world by choosing to play baseball. In 1986, this six-foot-one tall, 222-pound athlete joined the Kansas City Royals and became their regular left fielder in 1987. At the end of the 1987 season, he astonished the sports world again by declaring he would play for the Los Angeles Raiders for the rest of their football season. He announced that professional football was like a "hobby" to him, and he continued to report late to the National Football League. His contract with the Raiders provided for a ten-day break after the conclusion of the Royals' baseball season. He was the first athlete to be named to the All-Star squad in both professional football and professional baseball. But on January 13, 1991, during a playoff game with the Cincinnati Bengals, he sustained what may have been a career-ending injury to his hip. Dropped by the Royals, he was picked up as a DH by the White Sox. Things still did not go right, and in March of 1992 the Sox put him on waivers, not so much to get rid of him, but rather to resign him to a new contract without exercising his $910,000 option. That same month, the superstar decided to have a hip replacement. On April 4, surgeons gave him his new artificial hip, and perhaps there was hope that he would make a comeback.

VIC JANOWICZ: FINALLY A FOOTBALLER

Vic Janowicz, the five-foot, nine-inch tall halfback for Ohio State (1950) and Heisman Trophy Winner, chose to play professional baseball. Primarily a catcher, he played for the Pirates (1953–1953), but batted only .214 in 83 games, and decided to switch to professional football. In 1954 and 1955, he played for the Washington Redskins and led the team in rushing (397 yards) and scoring (88 points on seven touchdowns, six field goals, and 28 points after touchdowns).

THE NEON MAN

A baseball/football star who has caught the attention of all sports fans today is "Neon" Deion Sanders. He leans toward football with the Atlanta Falcons, but he also plays for the Atlanta Braves. In 1991 he took practice with the Falcons and played a night game with the Braves that evening. In 1992, on September 17, he played for the Braves and took a plane to Miami, where he played for the

Falcons. Sanders decided to stay with the Braves for the World Series, in which he hit .533, getting eight hits and scoring four runs. To illustrate his importance to both teams, here is an example of a unique day in his life. Sanders left the Braves in late summer 1991, when the Falcons started training camp. After the fourth game of the football season, on September 21, he had been named the defensive player of the week in the NFL for his part in the defeat of the Los Angeles Raiders, 21–17. Then came an urgent request from the Braves, who were in the thick of the National League West pennant race. The Braves had just lost their leadoff man, Otis Nixon, who was leading the major leagues in base stealing with 60, and they needed some help from the fleet-footed Sanders. He spent the morning of September 25 at football practice. He went through calisthenics, catching drills, and pass coverage drills. Then he showered and went to a Falcons team meeting. Usually he would go home after all this and take a nap. But not this time. After the team meeting broke up, Sanders boarded a news helicopter from an Atlanta television station and sailed southward to downtown Atlanta, where he landed in a parking lot near the State Capitol. Once Sanders touched down, a television station car took him to the ballpark, where he arrived wearing a sweatsuit and carrying a football. There he was, ready for a baseball game on the same day he had practiced with his football team. In the first game of a doubleheader with the Cincinnati Reds, Sanders was inserted at first base as a pinch runner, and promptly stole second base. In 1992, with the Braves in another pennant race, he decided to remain with them until the end of the season.

JIM THORPE: OLYMPIC STAR

Jim Thorpe, whose Indian name was Bright Path, attended the Carlisle, Pennsylvania Indian Industrial School, where he was an all-around athlete. This six-foot tall, 200-pounder played minor-league baseball for Rocky Mount and Fayetteville, North Carolina in the Eastern Carolina League in 1909 and 1910. In 1912, he went to the Olympic Games in Stockholm, Sweden, where he was the first person to win both the decathlon and the pentathlon. Later, officials took back his Olympic medals after discovering that he had been a professional baseball player. Thorpe then played the outfield for the

Giants 1913–1915), the Reds (1917), the Giants again (1917–1919), and the Boston Braves (1919), batting .252.

In 1919, Thorpe left baseball to play professional football, which had just begun. He played in the backfield for the Canton Bulldogs (1919–1920), the Cleveland Indians (1921), the Oorang Indians of Marion, Ohio (1922–1923), the Toledo Maroons (1923), the Rock Island, Illinois Independents (1924), the New York Giants (1925), and the Bulldogs again (1926). In many of those years he was player-coach. Thorpe was elected to the Pro Football Hall of Fame in 1963.

A DREAM FIELD

In 1989, *Field of Dreams* was nominated for the Academy Award for best picture. It was a warm, nostalgic baseball movie that became everybody's favorite father-son reconciliation saga. Ray Kinsella (Kevin Costner), a down-to-earth, likeable Iowa farmer, feels that he might be becoming stodgy. He hears a mysterious voice telling him, "If you build it, he will come." Then a vision shows him a baseball diamond in the middle of his corn field.

The baseball field built by Universal Studios for the picture at a cost of about $5 million was created outside Dyersville, Iowa, a small town northeast of Iowa City, and it straddled a property line between two farms.

After the film was shot, Don Lansing, the farmer who owned right field and most of the infield, proved to be rather sentimental. He kept the grass trimmed and his part of the field in repair. Al Ameskamp, who owned left and center field, tore out the sod and planted corn again. But true to the voice's prediction, people began to come, and Ameskamp relented. Today, visitors can see a white farmhouse with a picket fence in front on a hillock above the baseball field. Little wooden bleachers sit behind the first base line, and in the summer the outfield fence is a two-acre field of corn.

There is no admission charge or tour guide, and the field is free to anyone who wants to use it for a game. There is a small souvenir stand on the third base side of the field, and a stand behind home plate, plus an unmanned donation box. Visitors even can take an ear of corn from the farms at no charge. It has been estimated that some 65,000 people come to see the field each year.

STAND FOR YOUR TEAM

Even people who have never been to a baseball game may have seen Harry Caray, the broadcaster of the Chicago Cubs games on television, stand in the seventh inning to sing "Take Me Out to the Ball Game" to cheer his Cubbies on. The seventh-inning stretch has become a part of the game wherever it is played. But where and when did the practice start?

For years it was thought that President William Howard Taft, whose tenure ran from 1909 to 1913, was the cause of the ceremony. (See "Baseball and U.S. Presidents" on page 199 for the traditional explanation.) But that may not be true.

In June of 1869, *The New York Herald* reported on a game between the Cincinnati Red Stockings and the Brooklyn Eagles: "At the close of the long second inning, the laughable stand up and stretch was indulged in all round the field." And later that year, the *Cincinnati Commercial* told of a break in a game between the Red Stockings and the Eagle Club of San Francisco: "One thing noticeable in this game was a ten minutes' intermission at the end of the sixth inning—a dodge to advertise and have the crowd patronize the bar."

In June of 1882, during a game between Manhattan College and the New York Metropolitans, a Christian Brother named Jasper Brennan, who was Manhattan's coach, noticed that his team was becoming restless on the bench. When it was their turn to bat in the seventh inning, he encouraged the students to stand up and stretch.

Then came the first game of the 1889 championship series between the New York Giants of the National League and the Brooklyn Bridegrooms of the American Association. *The Sporting News* reported: "As the seventh opened, somebody cried, 'Stretch for luck!' And instantly the vast throng on the grand stand rose gradually and then settled down, just as long grass bends to the breath of the zephyr." That was 20 years before Taft took office.

Doctoring the Ball—Legally

As far as baseball pitchers have been concerned, brand-new baseballs direct from the factory have always been too slick to be gripped properly. The remedy in the good old days was to rub them down with a combination of home plate dirt and tobacco juice. But the problem with this method was that the dirt produced scratches in the horsehide, causing some pretty wobbly pitches. And the tobacco juice made irregular stains that made it more difficult for the batter to follow the path of the ball.

For the last 50 years or so, the answer to the problem has been a kind of gunk called Lena Blackburne Baseball Rubbing Mud. All major league teams, plus some minor league teams, use the stuff to make the ball more grippable.

Lena Blackburne was not a woman. He was a man who had been a White Sox shortstop and later a coach with the old Philadelphia Athletics. He developed a "secret formula" to remove the slipperiness from new baseballs. According to Burns Bintliff, the man who inherited the formula after Blackburne died, "You just dab some mud on and rub it all over the ball. It takes the gloss off without scoring the surface."

This gooey, blackish-brown stuff is as thick as cold cream, and is collected in southern New Jersey every autumn. Bintliff won't tell exactly where his mud mine is, and he certainly won't tell what he does with the mud to make it more smooth so that it doesn't scratch the ball. He won't even tell the price he charges. But he does admit that he stores it over the winter in plastic garbage cans.

All winter long his neighbors deliver empty coffee cans to his door, and in the spring, Bintliff packs the mud into the cans and seals them with duck tape. Then he sends them off to every major league club. The standard order is 15 pounds per team, although some of them need a bit more.

"I'm not getting rich," Bintliff says. "In fact, I'm probably losing money on it. But I'm not doing it for the money. I'm doing it for the love of baseball." His efforts will be remembered. There is a can of Lena Blackburne's Rubbing Mud in the Baseball Hall of Fame in Cooperstown, New York.

The Cartwright Rules

Alexander Joy Cartwright, Jr. was a young man who, early in the nineteenth century, played the English game of rounders and other contests involving a ball and bases. By 1842, when he was 22, he was one of a group of young New York men who played a new game called "base ball." By 1846, Cartwright had set up a new set of rules for the game, dropping the rounders regulations that provided for a runner to be retired by being hit with a thrown ball. The new rules provided for foul lines, nine players to a team, and nine innings to a game. Here are the regulations that the "Father of Baseball" laid down.

1. Members must strictly observe the time agreed upon for exercise, and be punctual in their attendance.
2. When assembled for practice, the President, or in his absence, the Vice-President, shall appoint an Umpire, who shall keep the game in a book provided for that purpose, and note all violations of the By-Laws and Rules during the time of exercise.
3. The presiding officer shall designate two members as Captains, who shall retire and make the match to be played, observing at the same time that the players put opposite each other should be as nearly equal as possible; the choice of side to be tossed for, and the first in hand to be decided in a like manner.
4. The bases shall be from "home" to second base, forty-two paces; from first to third base, forty-two paces, equidistant. [Forty-two paces equals 90 feet.]

5. No stump match shall be played on a regular day of exercise.

6. If there should not be a sufficient number of members of the Club present at the time agreed upon to commence exercise, gentlemen not members may be chosen in to make up the match, which shall not be broken up to take in members who may afterwards appear; but in all cases, members shall have the preference, when present, at the making of a match.

7. If members appear after the game is commenced they may be chosen in if mutually agreed upon.

8. The game is to consist of twenty-one counts, or aces, but at the conclusion an equal number of hands must be played.

9. The ball must be pitched, and not thrown, for the bat.

10. A ball knocked out of the field, or outside the range of the first or third base, is foul.

11. Three balls being struck out and missed and the last one caught is a hand out; if not caught is considered fair, and the striker is bound to run.

12. A ball being struck or tipped and caught either flying or on the first bound is a hand out.

13. A player running the bases shall be out, if the ball is in the hands of an adversary on the base, or the runner is touched with it before he makes his base; it being understood, however, that in no instance is a ball to be thrown at him.

14. A player running who shall prevent an adversary from catching or getting the ball before making his base, is a hand out.

15. Three hands out, all out.

16. Players must take their strike in regular turn.

17. All disputes and differences relative to the game, to be determined by the Umpire, from which there is no appeal.

18. No ace or base can be made on a foul strike.

19. A runner cannot be put out in making one base, when a balk is made by the pitcher.

20. But one base allowed when a ball bounds out of the field when struck.

Baseball and U.S. Presidents

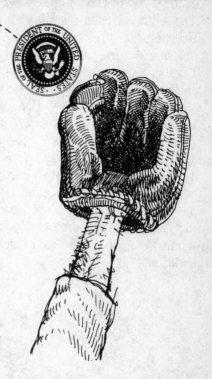

There have been ten presidents who played baseball in their youth—Ulysses S. Grant, Benjamin Harrison, William Howard Taft, Woodrow Wilson (who also briefly coached the football team at Wesleyan University), Herbert Hoover (who also managed the football team at Stanford University), Dwight D. Eisenhower, John F. Kennedy, Jimmy Carter (who preferred softball), Ronald Reagan, and George Bush.

Taft was the first presidential baseball fan. He was the first chief executive to throw out the first ball to open the baseball season (Carter was the first president to break that tradition). In 1910, he arrived at the ball park to see the Washington Senators' home opener against the Philadelphia Athletics, and was asked by umpire Billy Evans to do the honors. Later that year, Taft was in St. Louis and found that both the Cardinals and the Browns were at home. Not wanting to offend either club, he saw parts of both games at Robinson's Field (Cardinals) and Sportsman's Park (Browns).

Taft may have been responsible for beginning another baseball tradition. The story says he was attending a game in Pittsburgh, and rose to stretch in the middle of the seventh inning. The crowd, thinking he was leaving, got up to honor him. Taft sat down, the crowd sat down, and the seventh-inning stretch was born.

Ronald Reagan was deeply involved in baseball. His first professional job was as an announcer on radio station WOC (the letters stood for World of Chiropractic) in Davenport, Iowa. The job paid five dollars a week plus bus fare. He went on to become a sportscaster for WHO in Des Moines, Iowa, where he was paid $75 a week. The job involved recreating Cub games as they came in over the ticker tape.

When Reagan got to Hollywood, he played baseball with the Leading Men, a baseball team made up of actors. In a 1949 charity game against the Comedians, he hit a grounder toward the shortstop, comedian Donald O'Connor. Seeing that the play would be close, Reagan slid in feet first, suffering a multiple fracture of the right thigh which took more than a year to heal.

But he still had a soft spot in his heart for the Cubs. In October 1988, he was in Chicago to make a speech and decided to go to Wrigley Field to watch a game. He ended up throwing out the first ball and doing the play-by-play on television for part of the first inning and all of the second. He later said, "You know, in a few months I'm going to be out of work, and I thought I might as well audition."

The most skillful ball player of all was President George Bush. When he was in prep school at Andover he was named Best Athlete at the school. Then he went on to Yale, where he became the regular first baseman on the baseball team in his junior year (1947), batting right and throwing left, with a batting average of .264. The team went on to the finals of the NCAA tournament, losing the national championship two games to none to the University of California. The next year he was captain of the Yale team that went to the finals of the NCAA tournament, losing to Southern California, two games to one.

His coach, Ethan Allen, said of him, "If you told him to bunt, he bunted." And Dodger scout Whitey Piurek said of his play in the NCAA's, "By professional standards, he wasn't a prospect. He could run, but he lacked real power."

Gehrig's Famous Farewell

Yankees first baseman Lou Gehrig replaced an ailing Wally Pipp in the lineup on June 25, 1925, and he was to go on to accumulate the most amazing record in major league baseball history—appearing in 2,130 consecutive games. Along the way, he hit 23 grand slam home runs and had a career batting average of .340.

In 1938, his batting average dropped to .295, and it was obvious that he was sick. He had lost weight, and seemed to be losing his muscle tone. In 1939, he opened as usual at first base, but after collecting only four hits in his first eight games, Gehrig, as team captain, asked to speak to Manager Joe McCarthy. "I think I'm hurting the team," he said. "Maybe it would be better if I took a rest for awhile." So he benched himself on May 2, 1939. Babe Dahlgren took over first, and Gehrig never took the field again.

Gehrig entered the Mayo Clinic in Rochester, Minnesota, in June, and the tests showed that he was suffering from an incurable disease, amyotrophic lateral sclerosis—now often referred to as "Lou Gehrig's Disease." He was given two years to live. On July 4, 1939, the Yankees held Lou Gehrig Day in Yankee Stadium before 61,808 fans.

Gehrig' gave a memorable speech: "Fans, for the past two weeks you have been reading about a bad break I got. Yet today I consider myself the luckiest man on the face of the earth. I have been in ball parks for 17 years, and I have never received anything but kindness and encouragement from you fans. Look at these grand men [his teammates and former teammates, including Babe Ruth]. Which of you wouldn't consider it the highlight of his career just to associate with them for even one day? Sure I'm lucky. Who wouldn't consider it an honor to have known Jacob Ruppert? Also, the builder of baseball's greatest empire, Ed Barrow? To have spent six years with that wonderful little fellow, Miller Huggins? Then to have spent the next nine years with that outstanding leader, that smart student of psychology, the best manager in baseball history, Joe McCarthy? Sure I'm lucky. When the New York Giants, a team you would give your right arm to beat, and vice versa, sends you a gift—that's something. When everybody down to the groundskeepers and those boys in white coats remember you with trophies—that's something. When you have a wonderful mother-in-law who takes sides with you in squabbles against her own daughter—that's something. When you have a father and mother who work all their lives so that you can have an education and build your body—it's a blessing. When you have a wife who has been a tower of strength and shown more courage than you dreamed existed—that's the finest I know. So I close in saying that I might have had a bad break, but I have an awful lot to live for."

The Yankees retired Gehrig's uniform number that year—the first Yank ever to be so honored. Lou Gehrig died June 6, 1941 in Riverdale, New York. In 1989 the United States Postal Service issued a Lou Gehrig commemorative stamp.

Equipment and Rule Changes

Over the years, there have been many changes in the rules and the equipment for the game of baseball, but few of them have violated the original intent of the Cartwright rules. Here are a few of the more important ones.

1845—The ball is required to weigh three ounces. The pitching distance is to be 45 feet.

1854—The weight of the ball is increased to between 5½ to 6½ ounces and it must be 2¾ to 3½ inches in diameter.

1859—Bats are to be no more than 2½ inches in diameter.

1860—Whitewash is to be used to mark the foul lines.

1863—Bats must be round and made of wood

1868—The bat is to be no more than 42 inches long.

1869—The pitcher's box is to be a six-foot square.

1872—The ball is to weight not less than five or more than 5½ ounces. The ball's circumference is to be not less than nine or more than 9¼ inches.

1875—The unpadded glove may be used.

1877—The bases are to be canvas-covered. The bases are to be 15 inches square. Home plate is to be located just within the diamond at the intersection of the first and third baselines.

1881—The pitcher's box is to be 50 feet from the plate.

1882—The three-foot baseline is to be used.

1883—The pitcher is allowed to pitch overhand.

1885—Home plate may be made of marble or whitened rubber. The bat may have one flattened side.

1886—The bat must be round. The pitcher's box is to be 4 feet x 7 feet. First and third bases are to be within the foul lines. Stolen base statistics are introduced and a runner is credited with a stolen base for each base advanced on another player's hit.

1887—A batter can no longer call for a high or low pitch. Home plate must be made of rubber and must be a 12-inch square. The pitcher's box must be 4 feet x 5½ feet. The number of balls for a walk will be five, rather than nine. A walk will count as a hit.

1888—The number of strikes for a strikeout will be three rather than five.

1889—The number of balls for a walk will be four rather than five.

1891—Substitutions other than for injury or with the permission of the other team are allowed.

1893—The pitcher's plate is to be made of rubber and the box is eliminated. The rubber is to be 12 inches x 4 inches The rubber is to be located 60 feet, 6 inches from home plate.

1895—Foul tips are to be counted as strikes. The pitcher's rubber is to be 24 inches x 6 inches. The bat diameter is to be 2¾ inches.

1898—Stolen bases are not to be given for advancing on a teammate's hit.

1900—The plate is to be five sided and 17 inches wide.

1901—Foul balls will be counted as strikes.

1903—A foul tip caught after two strikes will be an out.

1910—The ball will be cork-centered.

1920—The lively ball will be used, with its Australian yarn and tighter winding.

1926—The cushioned cork-center ball will be used.

1934—Both major leagues will use the same brand of baseball.

1950—The pitcher's mound will be a standard 15 inches higher than the baselines.

1954—The bat may be made of laminated wood.

1959—New baseball parks must be built with fences at least 325 feet down the lines and 400 feet in center field.

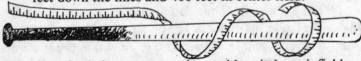

1962—Oversized gloves may not be used by pitchers, infielders, and outfielders. Players may used a grip-improving substance on their bats, but not for more than the first 18 inches beginning at the handle.

1968—The pitcher's mound will be ten inches higher than the baselines.

1971—Protective helmets will be used by batters.

1973—The American League may be use designated hitters.

1975—The ball may be made of cowhide or horsehide. Cupped bats may be used.

Food at the Ball Park

Americans have always had definite traditions when it comes to eating at the ball park. Take the hot dog, or frank, or red hot, depending on where you live.

There is a question as to when hot dogs were introduced to ball parks. There are those who claim that the owner of the St. Louis Browns, Chris von der Ahe, started selling them at Sportsman's Park one hundred years ago. Others think that Harry M. Stevens started selling them at the Polo Grounds in New York in 1900. He called them dachshunds, and sold them by yelling, "Get 'em while they're hot." It is said that Tad Dorgan, a cartoonist for the *New York Evening Journal,* was at the game, and he drew cartoon characters of the sausages, giving them tails and feet and the label "hot dogs."

There are variations on the plain old hot dog. Several ball parks in the Midwest offer bratwurst sandwiches. And there is the double dog sandwich to be found in Baltimore's Memorial Stadium, which is a sandwich with two franks in a bun that is cut twice, leaving a wall of bread between the two dogs.

Candy has baseball connections, too. But the chances are that the Baby Ruth candy bar was not named after the baseball player. However, the similarity of the names certainly didn't hurt sales. The commonly-accepted story is that it was named in honor of a daughter of President Grover Cleveland. Then there was the Reggie! candy bar. When Reggie Jackson was with the Orioles, he said, "If I ever played in New York, they'd name a candy bar after me." Sure enough, he went to the Yankees and the candy bar appeared.

In 1989 came a Culinary revolution at the ball park. The San Diego Padres began to offer sushi (raw fish) in their concession stands. Not to be outdone, the San Francisco Giants began to sell yogurt, salads, and tofu hot dogs.

Some Crazies and Con Men

VOODOO IN SAN DIEGO

In 1988, the Astros lost 11 straight games at Jack Murphy Stadium in San Diego, and the losing pitcher of the 11th game, Jim Deshaies, decided to do something about it. He bought a book on witchcraft and performed a curse-breaking ceremony in the visitor's clubhouse. He took twigs from four different trees, spit on them, and threw them into a fire while chanting a curse. Deshaies asked his teammates if anyone didn't believe in the curse, and only first baseman Glenn Davis said yes. The Astros beat the Padres 4-1 that night, and Davis strained a hamstring muscle.

GLOVE BURNING

When Iona College pitcher Phil McKiverkin lost seven games in a row in 1988, he blamed his losing streak on his new glove, a Bret Saberhagen model. McKiverkin decided to perform an exorcism (a ceremony held to get rid of evil spirits). He poured alcohol all over the glove and set it afire along the left field foul line. His teammates helped by uttering incantations. The next day McKiverkin went in to relieve wearing a borrowed glove and got credit for a win over Brooklyn College. He was modest about it, saying, "I'm grateful to my teammates. They could have burned my right arm instead."

BIRD STREAK BROKEN

Baltimore disc jockey Mike Filippelli was a die-hard fan of the Orioles. In 1988, the Birds set a record by losing the first 21 games of the season. When they were halfway through the streak, Filippelli bet Vince Edwards, his broadcast partner, that the Orioles' streak would not reach 13, and the two let the listeners decide the punishment if the team did lose their 13th. The Orioles lost, Filippelli's punishment was to crawl and walk a 6.2-mile stretch of Maryland's Coastal Highway. It took him four hours. He also had to dress in an Orioles jersey and helmet, sit in a plastic kiddie pool, and have 30 gallons of chocolate syrup poured over him. Observers decorated him with cherries, pineapple, sprinkles, nuts, and whipped cream. Filippelli commented that it was "something not to tell my grandchildren about."

CHARLIE O

One of the strangest team owners was Charlie Finley. The owner of the Kansas City Athletics (he later moved the team to Oakland), he was the first to fit out his team in rainbow-colored uniforms. He also elected a mule (named Charlie O) to be the team mascot and installed a mechanical rabbit (named Harvey) which popped up from the ground to deliver new baseballs to the home plate umpire. He also brought sheep to Kansas City's Municipal Stadium and a shepherd to tend them. The sheep were put between the right field fence and the outer wall where they helped to keep the grass short.

VEECK MADNESS

Probably the most brilliant baseball team promoter of all time was Bill Veeck. In 1948, when he was the owner of the Indians, the club received a letter from a Cleveland baseball fan named Joe Earley, who claimed that he, an average fan, deserved a night in his honor. Veeck was intrigued with the idea, and on September 28, 60,405 fans showed up for "Good Old Joe Earley" Night. Earley, a 24-year-old night guard at an auto plant, was presented with a new convertible, clothing, luggage, books, and appliances. Other fans received livestock, poultry, and other gifts. Veeck spent $30,000 to have orchids flown in from Hawaii and gave one to the first 20,000 women entering the stadium.

On March 31, 1949, another crazed Indians fan, Charley Lupica, climbed a flagpole, sat on a platform at the top, and promised he would not come down until Cleveland was in first place in the American League. On September 25, Veeck had the platform moved to Municipal Stadium for a ceremony in which Lupica gave up his hopeless 117-day stunt. The team finished third that year.

Toward the end of the 1949 season, on September 23, Veeck, having realized that the Indians were out of the running after winning the World Series the year before, staged a funeral for the 1948 pennant. Wearing a top hat, he drove a horse-drawn coffin-containing hearse at the head of a funeral procession to the grave behind the center field fence. Manager Lou Boudreau and his coaches were the pallbearers, and the club's business manager read the last rites from *The Sporting News*.

Perhaps Veeck's most famous stunt occurred when he was the owner of the St. Louis Browns—the worst club in organized baseball. He hired a midget, Edward Carl "Eddie" Gaedel (1925–1961), who stood 43 inches and weighed 65 pounds. On August 19, 1951, Gaedel made his first and only appearance at the plate. The Browns were playing the Tigers, and Gaedel was sent in to pinch hit for outfielder Frank Saucier. Ed Hurley, the plate umpire, permitted him to bat when Zack Taylor, the Browns' manager, showed him a contract signed by Gaedel. Naturally, because of his tiny strike zone, Gaedel, wearing number ⅛, was walked in four pitches by pitcher Bob Cain. Gaedel was replaced by outfielder Jim Delsing, who ran for him. He never appeared again in the major leagues. Later, on opening day in in 1961, Gaedel and several other midgets served as vendors in the box seat section of Comiskey Park. Veeck, who now owned the White Sox, had received letters from fans complaining that the regular vendors were blocking their view.

On August 24, 1951, Veeck gave over 1,000 fans behind the Browns dugout YES and NO placards for the purpose of allowing them to have a part in the strategy of the game. The fans flashed the cards when asked by the coaches what the Browns should do. It worked. The Browns beat the Philadelphia Athletics, 5–3.

Baseball Cards

The baseball card, with its picture of a player along with his
personal statistics, is almost as
old as the professional game itself. One of the earlier distribu-
tors of baseball cards was the
maker of a cigarette called Sweet
Caporal. To get the card, a person had to buy a package of ciga-
rettes, and this so enraged
Honus Wagner, the future Hall
of Fame shortstop, that he de-
manded in 1909 that his cards
be destroyed. A nonsmoker, he
realized that young people were
the real baseball card collectors,
and he didn't want them to be
corrupted by the Sweet Caporal
people. In 1992, one of those
rare Wagner cards sold for
$451,000

Other companies got into the baseball card business. In 1932, the
U.S. Caramel Company had 32 cards printed, and offered a baseball ("value $1") for anyone who had a collection of all 32. But
hardly anyone could find card number 16, and for a while many
thought that the company was so stingy that they purposely didn't
print that card. In fact, card collectors didn't even know whose picture was on it. The mystery was solved in 1988. One number 16 was
found, and it had the picture of Hall of Fame Giant third baseman,
Freddie Lindstrom. Experts guess that it is worth $35,000.

The Topps Chewing Gum Company soon got into the production
of cards to package with their gum, and in 1952, they bought out
their chief rival, Bowman Gum. Topps pretty much had the field to
itself until 1981, when Fleer Corporation and the Donruss Company began to issue their own sets of cards. Then, in 1988, Major

League Marketing began to produce their own set under the name of Score.

Today, baseball cards are a big business. Dealers often buy and sell at top dollar, but they demand that the card be in almost mint condition. A 1952 Topps Mickey Mantle may go for $8,500, and a 1953 Topps Mickey Mantle is worth $1,400. A 1963 Topps Pete Rose can cost $550. The problem is that the real worth of a card depends on how much someone is willing to pay for it, and it can cost $1,500 to $2,000 just to get a collection started. Gone are the days when kids just flipped the cards in competitive games and then shoved them into a dresser drawer.

People can even collect umpire cards. In 1988, 100,000 sets of umpire cards went on sale at from $12 to $15 per set.

Baseball's Big Bucks

Paychecks for those who play the national pastime have ballooned since Harry Wright was paid $1,400 by the Cincinnati Red Stockings for the entire year of 1869. Many people were stunned when they learned that Babe Ruth was paid more than President Herbert Hoover in 1931. But baseball salaries today make all this look like small potatoes. In 1992, Ryne Sandberg, the Chicago Cubs second baseman, astonished the baseball world by signing a contract for $28.4 million over a period of four years. But it was not to begin until the 1993 season. That will be $7.1 million a year when it takes effect, and he will make much more when advertising endorsement money is figured in.

In 1992 the New York Mets were the big spenders, paying out $44.5 million in salaries, for an average of $1,711,615 per player. In all of baseball, only 36 players began the 1992 season making just the league minimum salary of $109,000, which is more than all but five state governors make per year. Of all players, 27.4 percent were signed for $2 million or more. Compare this with the salary of the president of the United States, who is paid $200,000 per year. Listed below are the players who signed for $2 million or more for the 1992 season:

NATIONAL LEAGUE

Atlanta Braves
Terry Pendleton, third base $3,000,000
Tom Glavine, pitcher $2,925,000
Charlie Leibrandt, pitcher $2,833,333
Ron Gant, outfielder $2,650,000
Alejandro Peña, pitcher................................$2,650,000
Sid Bream, first base...................................$2,400,000
Nick Esasky, first base $2,150,000

Chicago Cubs
Greg Maddux, pitcher $4,200,000
Andre Dawson, outfielder.............................$3,300,000
Mike Morgan, pitcher...................................$2,875,000
Danny Jackson, pitcher $2,625,000
Dave Smith, pitcher $2,500,000
Shawon Dunston, shortstop $2,475,000
Mark Grace, first base $2,262,500
Ryne Sandberg, second base $2,100,000

Cincinnati Reds
Barry Larkin, shortstop $4,300,000
Tom Browning, pitcher.................................$3,250,000
Jose Rijo, pitcher $3,083,333
Bill Doran, second base $2,833,333
Paul O'Neill, outfielder................................$2,833,333
Chris Sabo, third base $2,750,000
Greg Swindell, pitcher..................................$2,500,000
Tim Belcher, pitcher $2,100,000

Los Angeles Dodgers
Darryl Strawberry, outfielder $4,050,000
Tom Candiotti, pitcher..................................$3,750,000
Eric Davis, outfielder $3,600,000
Brett Butler, outfielder.................................$3,333,333
Orel Hershiser, pitcher..................................$3,333,333
Jay Howell, pitcher.......................................$2,575,000
Kal Daniels, outfielder..................................$2,500,000
Juan Samuel, second base.............................$2,325,000
Kevin Gross, pitcher $2,216,667

Roger McDowell, pitcher $2,200,000

Mike Scioscia, catcher....................................$2,183,333

Jim Gott, pitcher...$2,125,000

Montreal Expos

Dennis Martinez, pitcher $3,333,333

Ivan Calderon, outfielder...............................$2,600,000

New York Mets

Bobby Bonilla, outfielder $6,100,000

Dwight Gooden, pitcher $4,916,667

David Cone, pitcher.......................................$4,250,000

Eddie Murray, first base.................................$4,125,000

John Franco, pitcher $3,333,333

Vince Coleman, outfielder..............................$3,212,500

Bret Saberhagen, pitcher $3,050,000

Howard Johnson, third base $2,316,667

Tim Burke, pitcher $2,266,667

Sid Fernandez, pitcher $2,216,667

Philadelphia Phillies

Mitch Williams, pitcher $3,200,000

Dale Murphy, outfielder $2,500,000

Darren Daulton, catcher..................................$2,416,667

Len Dykstra, outfielder $2,316,667

John Kruk, first base......................................$2,300,000

Ken Howell, pitcher.......................................$2,000,000

Mariano Duncan, shortstop $2,000,000

Pittsburgh Pirates

Barry Bonds, outfielder..................................$4,700,000

Doug Drabek, pitcher $4,500,000

Andy Van Slyke, outfielder............................$4,250,000

Steve Buechele, third base $2,600,000

Zane Smith, pitcher $2,525,000

Jose Lind, second base $2,000,000

St. Louis Cardinals

Lee Smith, pitcher..$2,666,667

Jose DeLeon, pitcher.....................................$2,466,667

Pedro Guerrero, first base..............................$2,425,000

Andres Galarraga, first base $2,366,667

Bryn Smith, pitcher $2,233,333

Jose Oquendo, second base $2,050,000
Ozzie Smith, shortstop..................................$2,000,000

San Diego Padres
Fred McGriff, first base $4,000,000
Benito Santiago, catcher................................$3,300,000
Bruce Hurst, pitcher......................................$3,000,000
Tony Gwynn, outfielder $2,362,500
Randy Myers, pitcher $2,350,000
Tony Fernandez, shortstop $2,100,000
Craig Lefferts, pitcher $2,041,667
Larry Andersen, pitcher $2,000,000

San Francisco Giants
Will Clark, first base.....................................$4,250,000
Willie McGee, outfielder...............................$3,562,500
Dave Righetti, pitcher....................................$3,500,000
Bud Black, pitcher $2,750,000
Scott Garrelts, pitcher...................................$2,400,000
Billy Swift, pitcher $2,316,667
Kevin Bass, outfielder $2,000,000
Matt Williams, third base $2,000,000

AMERICAN LEAGUE

Baltimore Orioles
Glenn Davis, first base $2,865,000
Storm Davis, pitcher $2,566,667
Cal Ripken, Jr., shortstop..............................$2,100,000

Boston Red Sox
Frank Viola, pitcher......................................$4,733,333
Roger Clemens, pitcher..................................$4,555,250
Danny Darwin, pitcher $3,250,000
Mike Greenwell, outfielder $3,050,000
Jack Clark, DH $2,900,000
Wade Boggs, third base $2,700,000
Tom Brunansky, outfielder............................$2,700,000
Jeff Reardon, pitcher.....................................$2,633,333
Tony Pena, catcher $2,400,000
Ellis Burks, outfielder...................................$2,300,000
Matt Young, pitcher......................................$2,266,667

California Angels
Chuck Finley, pitcher $4,375,000
Mark Langston, pitcher $3,550,000
Bryan Harvey, pitcher $3,125,000
Gary Gaetti, third base $2,700,000
Lance Parrish, catcher $2,416,667
Hubie Brooks, outfielder $2,316,667
Von Hayes, outfielder $2,200,000

Chicago White Sox
George Bell, outfielder $3,650,000
Steve Sax, second base $3,575,000
Tim Raines, outfielder $3,500,000
Bobby Thigpen, pitcher...................................$3,166,667
Dan Pasqua, outfielder...................................$2,500,000
Kirk McCaskill, pitcher..................................$2,333,333

Detroit Tigers
Cecil Fielder, first base $4,500,000
Mickey Tettleton, catcher $3,333,333
Mike Henneman, pitcher $2,437,500
Alan Trammell, shortstop $2,400,000
Lou Whitaker, second base $2,200,000
Rob Deer, outfielder $2,016,667

Kansas City Royals
Wally Joyner, first base $4,200,000
Mark Davis, pitcher $3,625,000
Kevin McReynolds, outfielder.............................$3,416,667
Mike Boddicker, pitcher..................................$3,166,667
George Brett, DH...$3,100,000
Mark Gubicza, pitcher $2,666,667
Jeff Montgomery, pitcher $2,410,000

Milwaukee Brewers
Ted Higuera, pitcher $3,500,000
Paul Molitor, DH $3,433,333
Robin Yount, outfielder $3,200,000
Dan Plesac, pitcher......................................$2,766,667
B. J. Surhoff, catcher...................................$2,500,000
Bill Wegman, pitcher $2,375,000

Chris Bosio, pitcher $2,287,000
Franklin Stubbs, first base $2,166,667

Minnesota Twins
John Smiley, pitcher $3,440,000
Kent Hrbek, first base $3,100,000
Kirby Puckett, outfielder $2,966,667
Chili Davis, outfielder $2,800,000
Brian Harper, catcher $2,500,000
Rick Aguillera, pitcher................................$2,133,333

New York Yankees
Danny Tartabull, outfielder $5,300,000
Don Mattingly, first base..............................$3,620,000
Mike Witt, pitcher......................................$2,916,667
Matt Nokes, catcher....................................$2,500,000
Steve Farr, pitcher......................................$2,400,000
Tim Leary, pitcher $2,175,000
Jesse Barfield, outfielder $2,166,667
Roberto Kelly, outfielder..............................$2,150,000
Scott Sanderson, pitcher...............................$2,125,000

Oakland A's
Jose Canseco, outfielder $4,300,000
Mike Moore, pitcher $3,500,000
Dave Stewart, pitcher $3,500,000
Bob Welch, pitcher.....................................$3,450,000
Rickey Henderson, outfielder..........................$3,250,000
Dennis Eckersley, pitcher $3,000,000
Mark McGwire, first base..............................$2,650,000
Dave Henderson, outfielder $2,600,000
Ron Darling, pitcher $2,100,000
Terry Steinbach, catcher...............................$2,050,000

Seattle Mariners
Kevin Mitchell, outfielder.............................$3,750,000
Pete O'Brien, first base................................$2,187,500
Harold Reynolds, second base $2,166,667
Ken Griffey, Jr., outfielder $2,000,000

Texas Rangers
Ruben Sierra, outfielder $5,000,000

Nolan Ryan, pitcher $4,200,000
Rafael Palmiero, first base $3,850,000
Jeff Russell, pitcher $2,600,000
Julio Franco, second base $2,387,500
Bobby Witt, pitcher $2,383,333

Toronto Blue Jays

Jack Morris, pitcher $4,425,000
Joe Carter, outfielder....................................$3,666,667
Tom Henke, pitcher $3,666,667
Kelly Gruber, third base...............................$3,633,333
Dave Stieb, pitcher $3,250,000
Roberto Alomar, second base $2,833,333
Duane Ward, pitcher $2,425,000
Devon White, outfielder................................$2,333,333
Dave Winfield, outfielder $2,300,000
Jimmy Key, pitcher $2,275,000
David Wells, pitcher $2,063,000

Players Who Earned Between $1 Million and $1,999,999 in 1992

NATIONAL LEAGUE

Atlanta Braves

Lonnie Smith, outfielder................................$1,750,000
John Smoltz, pitcher $1,525,000
Mike Bielecki, pitcher $1,325,000
Jeff Treadway, second base............................$1,262,000
Juan Berenguer, pitcher $1,200,000

Chicago Cubs

Paul Assenmacher, pitcher $1,833,333

Cincinnati Reds

Billy Hatcher, outfielder................................$1,600,000
Bip Roberts, outfielder..................................$1,500,000

Rob Dibble, pitcher $1,400,000
Dave Martinez, outfielder $1,300,000
Norm Charlton, pitcher $1,100,000
Glen Braggs, outfielder.................................$1,000,000

Houston Astros
Ken Caminiti, third base $1,500,000
Craig Biggio, catcher $1,375,000
Mark Portugal, pitcher.................................$1,250,000
Steve Finley, outfielder.................................$1,120,000

Los Angeles Dodgers
Bob Ojeda, pitcher $1,600,000
John Candelaria, pitcher..............................$1,250,000
Tim Crews, pitcher.......................................$1,175,000
Todd Benzinger, first base $1,150,000

Montreal Expos
Tim Wallach, third base...............................$1,906,500
Spike Owen, shortstop..................................$1,333,333

New York Mets
Dave Magadan, first base $1,393,750

Philadelphia Phillies
Terry Mulholland, pitcher............................$1,250,000
Barry Jones, pitcher $1,025,000

Pittsburgh Pirates
Kirk Gibson, outfielder.................................$1,950,000
Mike Lavalliere, catcher...............................$1,850,000
Bob Walk, pitcher $1,225,000
Don Slaught, catcher $1,666,667

St. Louis Cardinals
Juan Agosto, pitcher $1,666,667
Milt Thompson, outfielder $1,666,667
Gerald Perry, first base $1,666,667

San Diego Padres
Kurt Stillwell, shortstop $1,750,000
Greg Harris, pitcher $1,025,000
Ed Whitson, pitcher $1,000,000

San Francisco Giants
Mike Jackson, pitcher...................................$1,666,667
Robby Thompson, second base $1,600,000

Jose Uribe, shortstop $1,533,333
Jeff Brantley, pitcher.....................................$1,125,000

AMERICAN LEAGUE

Baltimore Orioles
Gregg Olson, pitcher $1,450,000
Joe Orsulak, outfielder..................................$1,300,000
Rick Sutcliffe, pitcher....................................$1,200,000
Bob Milacki, pitcher $1,180,000
Randy Milligan, first base $1,050,000
Mike Devereaux, outfielder............................$1,000,000

Boston Red Sox
Joe Hesketh, pitcher......................................$1,775,000
Jody Reed, second base $1,600,000
Greg Harris, pitcher $1,400,000
Luis Rivera, shortstop....................................$1,075,000

California Angels
Jim Abbott, pitcher $1,850,000
Mark Eichhorn, pitcher $1,750,000
Luis Polonia, outfielder..................................$1,650,000
Dick Schofield, shortstop...............................$1,500,000
Chuck Crim, pitcher......................................$1,100,000

Chicago White Sox
Ozzie Guillen, shortstop $1,900,000
Jack McDowell, pitcher $1,600,000
Carlton Fisk, catcher $1,100,000

Detroit Tigers
Bill Gullickson, pitcher.................................$1,925,000
Frank Tanana, pitcher....................................$1,700,000
Tony Phillips, outfielder.................................$1,566,667
Eric King, pitcher $1,200,000
Dan Gladden, outfielder $1,050,000

Kansas City Royals
Jim Eisenreich, outfielder $1,650,000
Gregg Jefferies, second base $1,150,000
Neal Heaton, pitcher $1,100,000

Milwaukee Brewers
Ron Robinson, pitcher $1,100,000
Edwin Nunez, pitcher....................................$1,075,000

Jesse Orosco, pitcher.................................$1,075,000
Jim Gantner, second base $1,000,000

Minnesota Twins
Greg Gagne, shortstop $1,933,333
Mike Pagliarulo, third base $1,200,000
Shane Mack, outfielder $1,075,000
Bob Kipper, pitcher $1,000,000

New York Yankees
Mike Gallego, second base $1,950,000
Lee Guetterman, pitcher.............................$1,600,000
Greg Cadaret, pitcher $1,190,000
Melido Perez, pitcher $1,165,000
Mel Hall, outfielder $1,100,000

Oakland A's
Harold Baines, outfielder............................$1,583,333
Rick Honeycutt, pitcher $1,400,000
Gene Nelson, pitcher..................................$1,250,000
Willie Wilson, outfielder $1,000,000

Seattle Mariners
Dave Valle, catcher $1,866,667
Jay Buhner, outfielder $1,445,000
Randy Johnson, pitcher...............................$1,392,500
Erik Hanson, pitcher $1,345,000

Texas Rangers
Jose Guzman, pitcher $1,365,000
Kevin Brown, pitcher $1,200,000

Toronto Blue Jays
Ken Dayley, pitcher....................................$1,983,333
Candy Maldonado, outfielder.......................$1,250,000
Todd Stottlemyre, pitcher $1,200,000
Manny Lee, shortstop..................................$1,000,000

Average Player's 1992 Salary—Club by Club

Mets, $1,711,615
Dodgers, $1,613,821
Red Sox, $1,523,378

Padres, $1,091,951
Cubs, $1,076,327
White Sox, $1,075,494

Blue Jays, $1,504,368
Reds, $1,334,000
Yankees, $1,316,012
Royals, $1,300,060
A's, $1,295,511
Angels, $1,226,827
Pirates, $1,225,468
Braves, $1,136,548
Brewers, $1,130,302
Giants, $1,100,167

Tigers, $1,068,454
Twins, $986,173
Rangers, $949,861
Cardinals, $948,477
Mariners, $831,290
Phillies, $810,728
Orioles, $781,372
Expos, $572,617
Astros, $472,111
Indians, $286,917

The Language of Baseball

Baseball, like most sports, is a gold mine of colorful words and phrases. In fact, many of them have crept into the everyday language of American English. Here are a few of them.

Ace: The best pitcher on the ball team. The Cincinnati Red Stockings, the first professional team in the game, went 56–1 in $1869, and their only pitcher was Asa Brainard. Therefore, any pitcher who was outstanding was called an "Asa," which was soon shortened to "Ace."

Around the horn: When an out is made with no one on base, the opposing infielders throw the ball around the infield from third to first. This term was taken from the route that ships had to take around Cape Horn in South America before the Panama Canal was opened.

Boot: An error made while fielding a ground ball—this sometimes includes accidentally kicking the ball.

Bullpen: The place on the field where relief pitchers warm up. This word was used partly because of the Bull Durham tobacco ads painted on the outfield walls.

Can of corn: A fly ball easy to catch—from a grocer's practice early in the century of stacking cans on high shelves, to be tipped with a long stick and caught by the grocer.

Country-fair hitter (also pretty fair country hitter): A good hitter, taken from the strong farmers who played ball at fairs.

Ducks on the pond: The bases are loaded.

Farm team: A minor league club owned or subsidized by a major league team. The phrase came from the small rural towns where these minor league clubs played.

Holler guy: A player who continuously encourages his teammates.

Hot dog: A player who shows off.

Iron man: A durable ballplayer.

Out of left field: Unexpected. This phrase came about because of the vastness of the outfield and its distance from the infield.

Major league: The top level.

Minor league: Inferior.

Muff: To misplay the ball. The word came from the early baseball slang word, "muffin," meaning an inept player.

On deck: Next to bat, ready, waiting.

Pinch hitter: One who is used to take another batter's place. This is often used incorrectly in common speech, since a baseball pinch hitter is usually a better hitter than the man he hits for.

Play ball: To cooperate.

Play-by-play: A running commentary on the baseball action.

Rain check: The part of a baseball ticket to be used on another day if a game is rained out. Thus, a reinvitation to an event at some future time.

Rain out: A rain that is hard enough to cause postponement of a game. Thus, any lack of success.

Relieve: To take over for another player. Also, to take over another's job.

Root: To encourage a team. The word probably comes from the idea that a fan is rooted to his or her team.

Southpaw: A left-hander, especially a pitcher. Whenever possible, ball parks were built so that home plate was in the west. That way, the batter didn't have to stare into the afternoon sun. So a pitcher's left arm was on the south side as he stood on the mound.

Strike out: To be out after being charged with three strikes. Thus, any failure.

MORE BASEBALL WORDS AND PHRASES

There are also many words and terms that arose in baseball and are part of the National Game. Here are some.

Alley: The section of the outfield between center and left or center and right.

Aspirin: A fastball—so called because it looks as small as an aspirin.

Bag: A base. Bases are made of canvas bags.

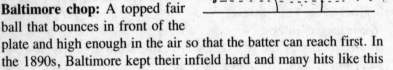

Baltimore chop: A topped fair ball that bounces in front of the plate and high enough in the air so that the batter can reach first. In the 1890s, Baltimore kept their infield hard and many hits like this were made.

Battery: The pairing of the pitcher and the catcher—after the military term for a group of big guns.

Bleachers: Unsheltered seats, usually beyond the outfield wall, so called because of the exposure to the sun.

Cleanup: The player fourth in the batting order who is powerful enough to drive runners home and "clean" the bases.

Collar: A batter who got no hits in a game once "wore the collar," since wagon horses' collars looked like zeroes.

Designated hitter or DH: A player who bats for the pitcher but does not play in the field.

Earned run: A run scored before the third out in an inning that is not the result of an error.

Earned run average: A statistic that tells the average number of earned runs given up by a pitcher for every nine innings.

Fireman: A relief pitcher who can "put out the fire" when he enters the game with men on base.

Fungo: A practice game in which a man throws a ball into the air and bats it himself to fielders. He uses what is called a fungo bat. There are three theories as to where the term came from. One says that in early versions of the game the hitter would recite the rhyme, "One go, two goes, fun goes." Or it may have come from the word "fungus," referring to the soft wood used in the fungo bat. It also might have come from the Scottish word, *fung*, which means "to toss."

Gopher ball: A pitched ball hit for a home run. Yankees' pitcher Lefty Gomez was the first to use the term, saying that bad pitches might "go fer" a home run.

Hit for the cycle: To hit a single, double, triple, and home run in a single game.

Hot corner: Third base, since the third baseman, often playing close to the batter, has to field many hard-hit balls.

Junior Circuit: The American League, since it was founded later than the National League.

Keystone sack: Second base, since it is the center of the infield.

Modern Era: In baseball, it is usually dated from 1903, when the two leagues played the first World Series.

Pepper: A practice game in which a player tosses the ball to a player who taps it to another player, who fields it and tosses it to other players.

Pull the ball: To hit the ball toward the outfield on the same side of the plate where the batter stands.

Ribby: Runs batted in—pronouncing the abbreviation RBI.

Rookie: A first-year player. The word comes from the army term, which was probably a shortened form of "recruit."

Rubber: The pitcher's mound, since it is made of rubber.

Screwball: A breaking ball that curves the opposite direction as a curve ball.

Senior Circuit: The National League, which was founded before the American League.

Slugging average: A statistic measuring extra base hitting. The total bases reached safely are divided by the total times at bat, carried to three decimal places.

Switch hitter: A player who can bat both right-handed and left-handed.

Texas leaguer: A ball softly hit just over an infielder's head, which falls in for a hit. In the 1890s, it was the specialty of Art Sunday of Toledo of the American Association, who had been a veteran of the Texas League.

Triple Crown: Won by a player who leads the league at the end of the season in batting average, home runs, and runs batted in.

Unearned run: A run scored after an error or interference call that should have caused the end of an inning. It is not charged against the pitcher in computing his earned run average.

Worm burner: A hit that skims along the ground.

Men of Courage

Over the years there have been countless baseball players who demonstrated more courage than the average person can comprehend. Hundreds of players have overcome bigotry, poor health, and physical handicaps. They are inspirations to all of us.

Blacks in Baseball

ALL-BLACK LEAGUES AND TEAMS

In 1867, history's first baseball league, the National Association of Base Ball Players, passed a resolution that barred blacks and the teams they played for from membership.

Even so, Moses Fleetwood Walker and his brother, Wilberforce Welday Walker, played for the American Association's Toledo club in the 1880s, and there were at least 20 blacks who played ball on mostly-white major league clubs. Before 1900, over 30 had played.

But in 1884, Chicago played an exhibition game with Toledo, and the Chicago manager, Cap Anson, saw Fleetwood Walker take his position, and bellowed a racist remark. Five years later he refused to play a Newark, New Jersey team that featured George Stovey, perhaps the best black pitcher of all time. In 1887, the New York Giants tried to bring Stovey up to the majors, but Anson was able to prevent it.

In 1901, the Orioles tried to sneak black second baseman Charlie Grant into the lineup by passing him off as a Cherokee Indian, but White Sox owner Charlie Comiskey made sure that this didn't happen. Similar events met similar fates.

These situation set a precedent that would last for many years, and was to force the creation of all-black teams and leagues. The National Negro Baseball League was formed in 1920, and it was followed by the Negro Eastern League and the Negro American League. Out of this came the Negro World Series.

PLAYERS SPEAK OUT

In addition to playing others in their own league, these black teams often played, and often beat, teams of white professionals in exhibition games. One of the early giants of black baseball, John Henry "Pop" Lloyd, was often compared to Honus Wagner. Wagner himself commented, "It's a privilege to have been compared to him." Wagner also considered Andrew "Rube" Foster, who pitched for the Chicago Lelands and later founded the National Negro Baseball League, "the smartest pitcher I have ever seen in all my years in baseball."

Yankees first baseman Lou Gehrig was to say, "I've seen many Negro players who should be in the major leagues. There is no room in baseball for discrimination. It is our national pastime and a game for all." Cubs catcher and later manager, Gabby Hartnett, agreed: "If managers were given permission, there'd be a mad rush to sign up Negroes." And Cardinals pitcher Dizzy Dean commented, "I have played against a Negro All-Star team that was so good, we didn't think we had an even chance against them." But these remarks were made during the 1930s, and baseball had years to go before the color line was broken.

ROBINSON BREAKS COLOR BARRIER

The player to break the color barrier, of course, was the immortal Jackie Robinson. On August 28, 1945, he was signed by the general manager of the Brooklyn Dodgers, Branch Rickey, and sent to the Dodgers' Montreal Royals farm club in the International League. Rickey tried to prepare him for what was going to happen once Robinson was brought up to the parent team:

"I want a ball player with guts enough not to fight back... I want you to know, Jackie, that there is no way for us to fight our way through this situation. There is virtually no group on our side. No umpires, no club owners, maybe a few newspapermen. We will be in a very tough spot. I have a great fear that there will be some fans who will be highly hostile to what we are doing. Jackie, it will be a tough position to be in, an almost impossible position. But we can win if we can convince everyone that you are not only a great ballplayer but also a great gentleman."

Robinson pointed out that this sounded like a battle. "Yes, exactly, a battle!" Rickey replied. "But it's one we won't be able to fight our way through. We have no army, no soldiers. Our weapons will be base hits and stolen bases and swallowed pride. Those will do the job and get the victory—that's what will win ... and, Jackie, nothing, nothing else will do it."

Robinson was called up to the Dodgers. Manager Leo Durocher was with the team at spring training in Panama, and he got wind of a players' strike against Robinson. He got the news after he had undressed to go to bed, but he dressed and called a late team meeting. "If you do this, if you have this strike," he told the men, "you can [expletives deleted]. He's a fine ballplayer, and he'll put money in your pocket and in my pocket, and he's going to play. And furthermore, *he's just the first. Just the first.*" Unfortunately, Durocher was fired for other reasons shortly afterwards.

Robinson did suffer hatred and bigotry. The whole St. Louis Cardinal team also threatened to strike just before the Dodgers were to open a series with them. National League President Ford Frick lost no time in setting the Cardinals straight. "You will find that the friends you think you have in the press box will not support you, that you all will be outcasts. I do not care if half the league strikes.

Those who do it will encounter quick retribution. They will be suspended, and I don't care if it wrecks the National League for five years. This is the United States of America and one citizen has as much right to play as another. The National League will go down the line with Robinson whatever the consequence. You will find if you go through with your intention that you have been guilty of complete madness"

Jackie Robinson went on to become one of the greatest players of all time, and blacks were now no longer outcasts. But breaking the color barrier was not over. In the National League, the Phillies were the last team to sign a black—John Kennedy, in 1957—ten years later. And it took 12 years for the Red Sox to sign Pumpsie Green in 1959. Not until the end of the 1974 season was Frank Robinson, the first black manager, chosen to be the skipper of the Indians. And it wasn't until 1989 that Bill White became president of the National League.

They Also Overcame

PITCHERS

HUGH DAILEY: One-Armed Hurler

Hugh Dailey was a pitcher who had one arm. He spent six years in the majors with several teams, from 1882 to 1887, winning 73 while losing 89 games. While he was with the Cleveland Spiders, he threw a 1-0 no-hitter against Philadelphia on September 13, 1883. He also struck out 16 men in one game at a time when four strikes were needed for a strikeout.

TOAD RAMSEY: Accident Victim

Toad Ramsey of the Louisville Colonels and the Cardinals won 114 games and lost 124 in his six years of play. His best years were 1886 (38-27) and 1887 (37-27, leading the league in strikeouts with 355). Ramsey had a disfigured pitching hand. He had been a bricklayer and cut through the tendon of his index finger with a trowel. Later, that liability became an asset, because he had a natural knuckleball, although the pitch was unknown in his day.

MONTY STRATTON: Comback Kid

Monty Stratton pitched for the White Sox from 1934 to 1938. He was one of the rising stars of the American League, winning 15 games in 1937 and another 15 in 1938. In November of 1938, a hunting accident caused the amputation of his right leg. But, wearing an artificial leg, he made a comeback in the minor leagues, and won 18 games in 1946 for Sherman in the East Texas League.

BERT SHEPARD: War Hero

Bert Shepard of Dana, Indiana, had been a fighter pilot in World War II whose plane was shot down. After the amputation of his right leg below the knee, he had a tryout with the Washington Senators. Wearing an artificial leg, he pitched against the Red Sox on August 4, 1945, and went 5½ innings, giving up three hits and one run.

HERB SCORE: Comeback Miracle

On May 7, 1957, pitcher Herb Score of the Indians was struck in the right eye by a line drive off Gil McDougald of the Yankees. He almost lost the sight in that eye, but came back in 1958, and won 17 games for the Indians and the White Sox before he retired in 1962.

BOB OJEDA: Amazin' Met

Late in the 1988 season, Bob Ojeda, then a Mets pitcher, nearly cut off part of a finger on his pitching hand in a freak accident with a power hedge trimmer in his garden. After microsurgery and a lot of physical therapy during the off season, he came back to start for the Mets in 1989, going 13–11, with a 3.47 ERA.

JIM ABBOTT: Olympian Achiever

Jim Abbott first gained the public's attention as a one-handed pitcher for the University of Michigan. He was born without a right arm, yet he was able to be a baseball star. Abbott was the winner of the 1987 Sullivan Award as the nation's top amateur athlete, and was winning pitcher in the final game of the 1988 Olympics, which gave the American team the gold medal. He had said, "I don't think people should make too much of it. I was blessed with a good left arm and a not so good right one. I don't think of myself as different, I don't think of myself as courageous. I grew up learning to do things within my capabilities. I've had a good time doing what I've done." Abbott was drafted in the first round by the Angels in 1988, and won 12 while losing 12 in 1989, with an ERA of 3.92. Then it was 10–14 (4.51) in 1990; 18–11 (2.89) in 1991; and 7–15 (2.77) in 1992. Late in 1992 he joined the New York Yankees.

OUTFIELDERS

DUMMY HOY: Brilliant Outfielder

William Ellsworth "Dummy" Hoy was a sterling outfielder for many clubs in his 14-year career although he was born hearing and speech impaired. He had a lifetime batting average of .288, and was a brilliant fielder and baserunner even though he was totally deaf. This was also in the days (1888–1902) before hand signals were used by managers, coaches, and umpires.

PETE GRAY: Expert Fielder

Born Peter J. Wyshner, Pete Gray played for the Browns in 1949, although he had lost his right arm in a childhood accident, retaining only a stub above the elbow. When he caught a ball in the outfield, he would throw the ball up in the air, throw the glove off his hand, catch the ball, and throw it back into play. In his 77 games in the majors, he batted .218 before he returned to the minor leagues, retiring in 1950. When asked how good he might have been if he had had two arms, he said, "Who knows? Maybe I wouldn't have done as well. I probably wouldn't have tried as hard and practiced as much as I did. And I probably wouldn't have been as determined."

Other Leagues

It has been said: toss a ball to a European, and he or she will kick it. Toss a ball to an American, and he or she will catch it and throw it. To a great degree, we owe that to baseball, since basketball and football came later. At any rate, baseball is designed to be played by people of all ages, all shapes, all sizes, and all degrees of proficiency. Here are some of the organizations that provide opportunities to play baseball.

The Minors

In the beginning, the minor league clubs were not deliberately organized. They were simply composed of teams in the smaller cities and particularly those cities outside the northeast quarter of the United States where the two major leagues were first based. Over the decades, many minor league teams were formed, but usually in their relationships to a major league club. At first, the minor league teams were totally independent clubs whose players would be under contract to them. To obtain these players, the major league teams would have to negotiate with the minor league teams.

THE "FARM CLUBS"

Gradually, more and more of the minor league teams came to be bought outright by the major league teams, or at least to have a working agreement under which the major league team would give some financial and instructional support in return for top priority in acquiring players. And it is because of this that the minor leagues have come to be regarded as "farm clubs," nurturing the young talents for the great harvest of the major leagues.

It was Branch Rickey who was the father of the high-powered use of the minor leagues to provide men for the majors. As the general manager of the Cardinals in the 1920s and 1930s, he sought out young talent, signed them to fairly cheap contracts, and placed them on minor league teams until they were ready to come to St. Louis or were sold to other teams. The other clubs soon followed suit.

ALPHABET DIVISION

At one time the minors were divided into seven classes, but in 1963, they were reorganized into four: AAA (or Triple A), AA (or Double A), A, and Rookie (limited to players in their first or second season of professional play). By the 1970s, the many minor league teams were organized into various leagues. Now, Class AAA has the American Association, the International League, the Pacific Coast League, and the Mexican League. Class AA has the Eastern League, the Southern League, and the Texas League. Class A has the Appalachian League, the California League, the Carolina League, the Florida State League, the Midwest League, the New York–Pennsylvania League, the Northwest League, the Pioneer League, the South Atlantic ("Sally") League, and three Mexican leagues.

Each season, minor league teams are allowed to draft players from the class below, and the major league teams are also allowed to bring up players at set times during the year.

During the 1930s and 1940s there were some 60 minor leagues with teams in over 400 cities in the United States, Mexico, and Cuba. But, with the advent of television sports and the spreading of the major leagues from coast to coast, they went into decline, and in the 1980s, there were only a few more than 140 minor league teams.

Little League

The Little League is not the old-est program for young amateur ballplayers, but it certainly is the most famous. It was begun in 1939 by Carl E. Stotz of Wil-liamsport, Pennsylvania, who decided that boys from about the ages of eight through 12 would benefit from more orga-nized games of baseball. Only three teams in Williamsport played that year, and it cost only $35 to buy uniforms for the three clubs. The idea spread, and in 1940, another team was formed.

World War II put a slight damper on the program, but by 1946, there were 12 leagues in the system, all of them in Pennsylvania. When the war was over, Americans turned to baseball with renewed enthusiasm, and Little League began to take off. In 1947, the Ham-monton, New Jersey, Little League became the first league estab-lished outside the state of Pennsylvania. That same year, the first Little League World Series was played in Williamsport, and it was won by the Maynard Little League team of Williamsport.

WORLD SERIES SPURS GROWTH

The publicity from that first series in 1947 greatly stimulated the growth of the Little League, and by 1948, there were 94 leagues with 416 teams. In 1949, the number almost doubled, and by 1950, there were 307 leagues. In 1951, there were 776, and the first Little League outside the United States was founded in British Columbia in Canada.  By 1952, there were over 1,500 programs, and in 1953, the World Series was televised by CBS, with sportscaster Howard Cosell giving the play-by-play on radio.

A most unusual thing happened after the 1992 World Series. Zamboanga City of the Philippines had beaten Long Beach, California 15–4 in the championship game, but it was found that the Filipinos had used eight ineligible players, and the California team was awarded the championship by the 6–0 score of a forfeited Little League game.

The number of leagues rose to more than 3,000 in 1954, and by 1955, Little League baseball had spread to all of the states. In 1959, with the number of leagues up to over 5,000, President Dwight D. Eisenhower proclaimed the first National Little League Week in the second week in June. In 1960, Little League baseball had 5,500 leagues, the game had spread to Europe, and a team from West Berlin, Germany, appeared in the World Series.

ORIGINAL IDEA EXPANDS

Eventually, in 1961, Little League was so popular that it expanded to sponsor teams for boys aged 13 to 15. By this time the program had spread to South America and the Far East. In 1968, Big League Baseball for players 16–18 was started, and there were more than 6,000 programs in the system. Girls were permitted to participate in Little League.

By 1978, Little League had grown to include over 6,500 Little Leagues for nine- to 12-year-olds, 2,850 Senior Leagues for 13- to 15-year-olds, and 1,300 Big League programs for 16- to 18-year olds. Junior League Baseball was created for 13-year-olds in 1979.

By the 1980s, Little League could count over 14,000 leagues, with some 145,000 teams and about 2.5 million youthful participants in over 30 countries (almost half of the teams and participants being in the United States). In 1989, the first graduate of the Little League program to be elected to the Baseball Hall of Fame in Cooperstown was inducted—outfielder Carl Yastrzemski of the Red Sox.

WORLD SERIES CHAMPIONS

Since the beginning of the Little League World Series, the finals have always been played in the city of its birth—Williamsport, Pennsylvania. Here are the winners:

1947—Maynard Midgets of Williamsport, Pennsylvania
1948—Lock Haven, Pennsylvania
1949—Hammonton, New Jersey
1950—Houston, Texas
1951—Stamford, Connecticut
1952—Norwalk, Connecticut
1953—Birmingham, Alabama
1954—Schenectady, New York
1955—Morrisville, Pennsylvania
1956—Roswell, New Mexico
1957—Monterrey, Mexico
1958—Monterrey, Mexico
1959—Hamtramck, Michigan
1960—Levittown, Pennsylvania
1961—El Cajon, California
1962—San Jose, California
1963—Granada Hills, California
1964—Mid Island, Staten Island, New York
1965—Windsor Locks, Connecticut
1966—Westbury American, Houston, Texas
1967—West Tokyo, Japan
1968—Wakayama, Japan
1969—Taipei, Taiwan
1970—American, Wayne, New Jersey
1971—Tainan, Taiwan
1972—Taipei, Taiwan
1973—Tainan City, Taiwan
1974—Kao Ksiung, Taiwan
1975—Lakewood, New Jersey

1976—Chofu, Tokyo, Japan
1977—Li-teh, Taiwan
1978—Pin kuang, Pin-tung, Taiwan
1979—Pu-Tzu Town, Taiwan
1980—Long Kuong, Hua Lian, Taiwan
1981—Tai-chung, Taiwan
1982—Kirkland National, Kirkland, Washington
1983—East Marietta National, Marietta, Georgia
1984—Seoul National, Seoul, Korea
1985—Seoul National, Seoul, Korea
1986—Tainan Park, Taiwan
1987—Hua Lin, Taiwan
1988—Tai Chung, Taiwan
1989—Trumbull, Connecticut
1990—Taipei, Taiwan
1991—Taiwan
1992—Long Beach, California

In the Little League World Series of 1992, history was made on two fronts. The first was that the games were played on a round-robin format, which gave losers a second chance, since a team would have to be beaten twice in order to be knocked out of the competition. The second was that it was decided to have night games. The first Little League night game was played on August 24, 1992, and the Hamilton Square, New Jersey club beat Lake Charles, Louisiana, 5–0.

FAMOUS LITTLE LEAGUERS

The list of people who went from Little League to success in sports and other fields is almost endless. Perhaps the most outstanding baseball example was Carl Yastrzemski, the Red Sox outfielder, who was the first Little Leaguer to go on to be elected to the Baseball Hall of Fame. Some of the others include:

Bill Bradley (United States senator)
George Brett (Royals third baseman)
Joseph Campanella (actor)
Gary Carter (Expos catcher)

Vince Coleman (Mets outfielder)
Danny DeVito (actor)
Mike Ditka (Chicago Bears football coach)
Rollie Fingers (A's pitcher)
Doug Flutie (Calgary Stampeders quarterback)
Steve Garvey (Dodgers first baseman)
Mike Greenwell (Red Sox outfielder)
Tony Gwynn (Padres outfielder)
Orel Hershiser (Dodgers pitcher)
Kareem Abdul Jabbar (Los Angeles Lakers basketball player)
Tommy John (Yankees pitcher)
Davey Lopes (Dodgers second baseman)
Lee Mazzilli (Blue Jays outfielder)
Dale Murphy (Phillies outfielder)
Eddie Murray (Mets first baseman)
Brent Mussberger (ABC-TV sportscaster)
Jim Palmer (Orioles pitcher)
Dan Quayle (former vice-president)
Kurt Russell (actor)
Nolan Ryan (Rangers pitcher)
Ron Santo (Cubs third baseman)
Mike Schmidt (Phillies third baseman)
Don Schollander (Olympic Gold Medal swimmer)
Tom Selleck (actor)
Bruce Springstein (rock singer)
Mel Stottlemyre (Mets coach)
Don Sutton (Dodgers pitcher)
Al Trautwig (ABC-TV sportscaster)

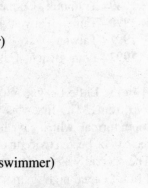

American Legion

Although Little League has become almost synonymous with organized baseball for young Americans, it was not the first such program. The American Legion Junior League was founded in 1925 to sponsor teams for teenagers up to the age of 17. The first national competition was held in 1926, and by 1929, there was at least one team representing each of the then 48 states.

In 1950, 18-year-olds were admitted, and the "Junior" was dropped from the official name. The program also spread to the two newest states, Alaska and Hawaii, as well as to Puerto Rico and the Panama Canal Zone. The program depends on the sponsorship of American Legion posts, so it cannot spread as far as Little League can. By the 1970s, there were some 3,200 teams in American Legion baseball involving boys from 16 to 18 years of age.

Other Youth Leagues

Several other programs sponsor baseball teams for young amateurs. The largest organization in the United States that sponsors amateur baseball teams for players of all ages is the American Amateur Baseball Congress (AABC), founded in 1935 as the American Baseball Congress (the "Amateur" was added in 1955), with its headquarters in Battle Creek, Michigan. Its program began with adult teams, but over the years it expanded to include five youth divisions: Pee Wee Reese (12 and under); Sandy Koufax (14 and under); Mickey Mantle (16 and under); Connie Mack (18 and under); and Stan Musial (19 and older). The AABC includes over 3,000 teams and has about 75,000 participants.

The Pony League (standing for Protect Our Nation's Youth) was founded in Washington, Pennsylvania, in 1950 for boys aged 13 and 14. A similar program, the Colt League, was founded in 1953 in Martins Ferry, Ohio, for boys aged 15 and 16. The Colt League merged with similar programs, and in 1959, joined with the Pony League to form Boys' Baseball, operating out of Washington, Pennsylvania. The organization later started a Junior League for boys aged eight to 12.

Another well-known program is the Babe Ruth League, which was originally called the Little Bigger League. It was founded in 1952 in Trenton, New Jersey, for boys aged 13 to 15.

In addition, some 15,000 American junior high and high schools sponsor at least one baseball team, with perhaps 500,000 participating young people.

Colleges and Universities

When the minor leagues began to die in the 1970s and 1980s, another source of baseball talent had to emerge. So the major league clubs turned their attention to the college and university baseball teams. For a long time these teams were virtually ignored at schools where thousands turned out for football and basketball games, but they began to attract serious players and spectators, as well as scouts from the major league teams.

Since 1963, organized baseball has supported summer leagues for promising undergraduates. And in 1947, the National Collegiate Athletic Association established a World Series for college baseball teams. The winners of this competition are as follows:

1947—University of California, Berkeley
1948—University of Southern California
1949—University of Texas
1950—University of Texas
1951—University of Oklahoma
1952—College of the Holy Cross
1953—University of Michigan
1954—University of Missouri
1955—Wake Forest University
1956—University of Minnesota
1957—University of California, Berkeley
1958—University of Southern California
1959—Oklahoma State University
1960—University of Minnesota
1961—University of Southern California
1962—University of Michigan
1963—University of Southern California

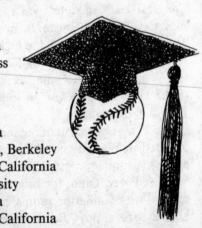

1964—University of Minnesota
1965—Arizona State University
1966—Ohio State University
1967—Arizona State University
1968—University of Southern California
1969—Arizona State University
1970—University of Southern California
1971—University of Southern California
1972—University of Southern California
1973—University of Southern California
1974—University of Southern California
1975—University of Texas
1976—University of Arizona
1977—Arizona State University
1978—University of Southern California
1979—California State University, Fullerton
1980—University of Arizona
1981—Arizona State University
1982—University of Miami
1983—University of Texas
1984—California State University, Fullerton
1985—University of Miami
1986—University of Arizona
1987—Stanford University
1988—Stanford University
1989—Wichita State University
1990—University of Georgia
1991—Louisiana State University
1992—Pepperdine University

Women's Baseball

On November 5, 1988, the Baseball Hall of Fame in Cooperstown, New York, finally recognized the fact that there have been women baseball players, too (over 550 of them), by opening a permanent exhibition called "Women in Baseball." It is a celebration of the All-American Girls' Professional Baseball League, which featured women's teams from 1943 to 1954.

The AAGPBL was founded late in 1942 by Philip K. Wrigley, the owner of the Chicago Cubs, who feared that major league play might be suspended during World War II. Of course, the major leagues never shut down, but the women's league provided good, hard-nosed baseball that hit a height of drawing nearly a million paying fans in its top year—1947.

The players, wearing their short-skirted uniforms, played real baseball, not softball—real baseball—hardball, overhand, stealing, sliding—for the following teams in the Midwest:

Battle Creek (Michigan) Belles
Chicago (Illinois) Colleens
Fort Wayne (Indiana) Daisies
Grand Rapids (Michigan) Chicks
Kalamazoo (Michigan) Lassies
Kenosha (Wisconsin) Comets
Milwaukee (Wisconsin) Chicks
Minneapolis (Minnesota) Millerettes
Muskegon (Michigan) Belles
Muskegon (Michigan) Lassies
Peoria (Illinois) Redwings
Racine (Wisconsin) Belles
Rockford (Illinois) Peaches
Springfield (Illinois) Sallies
South Bend (Indiana) Blue Sox

The regimen was strict, which was appropriate for those more innocent days. The women could not drink or smoke. They had to wear makeup on the field. They could not wear slacks or pants on or off the field. They were given grooming and deportment lessons. And their chaperone (every team had one) had to approve of any man who took a player out on a date.

The seasons were tough, and a series of baseball cards was printed for the women. The 15-team league played 115 to 127 games a season—often seven days a week with a doubleheader on Sundays. The players had to play hurt, since each team had a maximum of 15 players, with no minor league to furnish relief. No wonder Alice "Lefty" Hohlmayer McNaughton, a former Kenosha Comets pitcher and first baseman, recently put down modern male major leaguers with: "Boys today, they get a hangnail and they can't play."

For all this, the women were paid a small amount. In the beginning years they earned as little as $55 a week. Toward the end, they got as much as $125 per week.

Eventually, the league disappeared for lack of sponsorship. Then, too, the major league men had returned from the armed forces, and war-time gas rationing had ended and people could travel to see men play in the larger cities.

Only in 1992 were people reminded of the AAGPBL. The film *A League of Their Own* told a tiny bit of the story. And a book was published that chronicled the women of the diamond: *Girls of Summer: In Their Own League*, by Lois Browne.

There have been more than 125 father-son baseball-playing duos. But there has been only one example of a major league ballplayer who had a major league mother. Helen Callaghan St. Aubin, an outfielder for the Ft. Wayne Daisies, was once compared to Ted Williams for her hitting ability. Today, her son, Casey Candaele, plays second base for the Houston Astros.

The memory of one thing also remains. Despite the hullabaloo in 1988 when the Cubs finally installed lights for night games at Wrigley Field, history tells us that at least two AAGPBL games were played there in the mid-1940s at night, under temporary lights.

Pure Nostalgia

Without doubt, the strangest baseball league ever devised was the Senior Professional Baseball Association. It played one whole season, from November 1, 1989 to February 4, 1990. In the middle of its second season, it collapsed because of weak financial management.

The league was set up to feature former major league players, 35 and over (catchers could play at age 32). The teams were located in

Florida, where it was figured that retired people would be big fans. They weren't.

There were eight teams, and Curt Flood, the star outfielder of the St. Louis Cardinals, was named commissioner of the league. Among the managers were Earl Weaver (former Baltimore Orioles manager) of the Gold Coast Suns; Dick Williams (former Boston Red Sox, Oakland A's, California Angels, Montreal Expos, San Diego Padres, and Seattle Mariners manager) of the Palm Beach Tropics; Bill "The Spaceman" Lee (former pitcher for the Boston Red Sox and the Montreal Expos) of the Winter Haven Super Sox; and Bobby Tolan (former outfielder for the St. Louis Cardinals, Cincinnati Reds, San Diego Padres, and Philadelphia Phillies) of the St. Petersburg Pelicans.

Several former major league stars signed aboard, whether it was for the purpose of reliving old glories, making money, or in hopes of getting another chance at the big leagues, who can say? Among them were Vida Blue (former pitcher for the Oakland A's, San Francisco Giants, and Kansas City Royals); Graig Nettles (former outfielder/third baseman of the Minnesota Twins, Cleveland Indians, New York Yankees, San Diego Padres, Atlanta Braves, and Montreal Expos); Dock Ellis (former pitcher for the Pittsburgh Pirates, New York Yankees, and Texas Rangers); Luis Tiant (former pitcher for the Cleveland Indians, Minnesota Twins, Boston Red Sox, New York Yankees, Pittsburgh Pirates, and California Angels); Dave Kingman (former first baseman/third baseman/outfielder/DH for the San Francisco Giants, New York Mets, San Diego Padres, California Angels, New York Yankees, Chicago Cubs, and Oakland A's); and Juaquin Andujar (former pitcher for the Houston Astros, St. Louis Cardinals, and Oakland A's.)

For what it is worth, the first and only championship was won by the St. Petersburg Pelicans.

Foreign Leagues

Baseball was born in the United States, but it has become popular in other countries over the years. Part of this popularity stems from the fact that Americans have carried the game with them wherever they have gone, both in peace and in war. American servicemen, for example, have been playing the game among themselves for many years now, and in so doing have introduced the game to many people around the world. The American-based Little League has also spread the game among young people in many countries.

It seems natural that baseball would be played widely and well in our neighboring countries, Canada and Mexico. After all, their minor league teams have long fed players to the major leagues. There was even an attempt in 1946 by wealthy Mexicans to start a third major league, but it was quickly squelched by American organized baseball.

THE LATIN AMERICAN CONNECTION

Baseball has been extremely popular throughout Latin America and the Caribbean Islands, and not only in places where the United States has had direct contacts, such as in Puerto Rico, Panama, and the Virgin Islands. Baseball is popular in Venezuela, Nicaragua, and the Dominican Republic, and there is a lengthening list of players from those countries who have moved up to become prominent players in the major leagues. And during the winter in North America, it has long been the custom of many players in the major leagues to play with various Latin American teams, which, since 1947, have had their own Latin American championship series.

Cuba is a special case. Baseball was played there as early as 1878, and eventually Cuba supported a team, the Havana Cubans, which belonged to the Triple A International League. After Fidel Castro (who was good enough to have had a minor league contract offer to play baseball in the U.S.) took over as president, the United States severed diplomatic relations with Cuba in 1961, and thus cut off movement between the two countries. Now there are two independent leagues in Cuba, and baseball remains as popular as ever.

Then came the visit of an "all-star" team of American professionals in 1931 and the visit of Babe Ruth in 1934. Since then, the Japanese have embraced baseball. They now support two major leagues, the Pacific and the Central, each with six clubs that play 130-game seasons and play their own Japan Series. The games draw huge crowds. One difference, however, is that the teams in Japan are owned by big industrial companies, unlike the U.S. teams.

JAPAN CRAZY OVER BASEBALL

Baseball was introduced to Japan by Horace Wilson, an American teacher in Tokyo, in 1873. The sport caught on quickly and was supported by schools and universities, spurred on by occasional tours by American collegiate teams. Until the 1930s, baseball in Japan was an amateur sport, with the strongest teams coming out of the Japanese universities. To this day, the university teams remain as the "farm teams" for the professional leagues.

ACROSS THE ATLANTIC

Ever since World War II, when Italian youngsters saw American soldiers playing baseball during their brief recreational times, America's National Game has been popular in Italy. Today, this country is regarded as Europe's leading power in the game. But the Italians are not alone. In France, La Fédération Françoise de Baseball, de Softball et de Criket boasts some 270 baseball clubs with about 12,000 players. Just ten years ago, there were only 30 clubs with about 2,500 players.

While soccer and cricket are still the favorite team sports in England, there is a group called the London Baseball Association. The teams have been playing in Hampstead Heath, a huge park in London, for the last 15 years.

Baseball has yet to catch on elsewhere around the world as it has in Japan and in Latin America, but it is also played by semiprofessional teams in the Netherlands, Belgium, Spain, South Africa, Australia, Taiwan, and Tunisia. Baseball has truly become international.

Science at the Ball Game

Most baseball players don't realize it, but they are constantly being influenced by science and technology. Here are some explanations of how they have shaped the game of baseball.

HOW DOES A RUNNER ATTEMPT TO STEAL SECOND?

A runner on first base trying to steal second must get to second base during the time that it takes the pitcher to deliver the pitch and the catcher to catch the ball and throw it back to the second baseman or shortstop, who will attempt to tag out the runner.

Of course, the runner has taken a lead off first base. That means that the distance to be run has been cut down, which will shorten the runner's time in running from first to second base. And he will probably slide into second base.

WHAT'S THE PURPOSE OF A SLIDE?

Does it help a runner to get to second base any faster? Of course not. It does help him or her come in under the throw, but the opposing infielder is expecting that and will try to tag the runner low down. Actually, the runner is using the slide to slow down. Running flat out might cause him or her to run across second base, and the runner must stop there or he or she can be tagged out for not being on the base. The runner is really using the friction between the body and the ground to decrease acceleration and stop in a hurry.

WHY DOES A RUNNER ROUND THE BASES?

Inertia has been defined as the characteristic of all bodies that causes them to stay at rest, or to stay in constant motion. That is, unless an outside force acts upon the bodies. We have all experienced this when an automobile goes around a turn. Remember that objects tend to go in a straight line. If a turn is taken too fast without seat belts being fastened, we tend to slide right across the seat.

Now suppose a batter is trying to score an inside-the-park home run. The batter must run as fast as possible, so he or she does not run straight to first base, turn left, run straight to second base, turn left, etc. What must be done is called rounding the bases.

If he or she were to make a sharp turn at each base, it would be necessary to stop, then turn, and then head to the next base. There is no time for that, so the runner must follow a curved path around the infield, fighting inertia while keeping most of his or her speed. Running in a curved path is easier than stopping at each base and making a 90-degree turn toward the next base.

Think of how a runner tries to beat out an infield hit. He or she runs straight toward first base, trying to beat the throw. This is covering the shortest distance between home and first. But if he or she thinks there is a chance to stretch the hit into a double, the runner will follow a curved path toward first, therefore being in a position to make the turn toward second more effectively.

HOW DOES A PLAYER CATCH A HARD-HIT LINE DRIVE?

Newton's second law of motion says that the net force on a mass is directly proportional to, and in the same direction as, the acceleration of that mass. In other words, force = mass x acceleration, or F = ma. The mass stays the same, of course, so if the force increases or decreases, so will the acceleration. And if the acceleration increases or decreases, so will the force.

When an infielder catches a hard-hit line drive, he or she does it automatically. The ball is still traveling along an almost straight line, and it may even still be accelerating. What does the player do? Does he or she stand like a statue, holding the glove where he or she knows the ball will hit it? No. That would hurt.

Just as the ball hits the glove, the player moves his or her arm and hand back with the ball in the glove. And if the ball is a real screamer, the player's whole body may move backward. This is not because he or she is knocked back by the force of the ball.

What is happening is that the arm, hand, and body "give" a little bit, and this spreads the force of the ball hitting the glove over a greater span of time. The point is that when a ball is caught, its speed must be reduced to zero almost immediately. By having the hand give on impact, the player is increasing, by a fraction of a second, the time of reducing the speed to zero. The result is that the hand feels less shock and does not sting as much.

HOW DOES A PLAYER THROW A BALL TO MAKE IT GO FARTHER?

Everyone knows that the acceleration due to gravity is with us all the time. Drop a glass, and it will fall to the floor. Gravity acts on any thrown object, too. You know that your throw is eventually going to hit the ground, so if you want the ball to go farther, you have to keep it in the air longer, before gravity forces it to earth.

The way you do this is to increase the angle of your throw when you want it to carry a longer distance. Throwing to the plate from center field requires an arched throw, which will keep the ball in the air. If it is thrown flat, even with the same amount of force, it will hit the ground sooner.

But that doesn't mean that the pitcher, when throwing a fast ball the short distance to the catcher's mitt, can throw a flat ball. He or she, too, must put some arch in it, although not as much as the center fielder.

As soon as the ball leaves the pitcher's hand, gravity begins pulling it downward. Even the fastest pitcher's smoke ball may drop as much as 2½ feet by the time it reaches the catcher. That's why there is such a thing as a pitcher's mound. Even so, the pitcher must always aim a little higher than the point where he or she wants the ball to go. The pitcher knows that the ball will reach a point where its upward acceleration will be zero and the ball will start to drop.

By the way, the technicians have come up with a new kind of glove that might make throws to the infield more accurate. The idea is based on the premise that players are more accurate if they throw to a target. So a company has introduced black leather gloves with a target in them. The secret is that the palm part of the ball is left with its natural color, which is white, rather than tanning it dark gray. Since some positions are really "target positions," this is especially helpful when used in catchers' mitts and infielders' gloves for the first baseman, second baseman, and shortstop. Mets catcher Todd Hundley was one of the players who tested the new mitt, and he said, "The pitchers have seen it, and they really think it's going to help them with their concentration."

CAN PITCHING BE LEARNED?

Researchers Dr. Joe P. Bramhall, a team physician at Texas A&M University, and Dr. Charles Dillman of the American Sports Medicine Institute videotaped the deliveries of 48 major league pitchers, including Dwight Gooden, Nolan Ryan, Roger Clemens, and Dave Stewart. They found out that, although these men have different styles, they still, from a scientific point of view, were pitching in the same way.

As far as the arm angle, the elbow angle, the shoulder angles, and the balance were concerned, these men were doing the same things. The purpose of the study was to prevent young players from making mistakes that might lead to injuries of the pitching arm by learning the correct way to pitch.

The researchers came up with some rules.

1. In the wind-up, the pitcher should be balanced at the top of the leg kick, coiled, and ready to spring forward.
2. The length of the stride should be slightly less than the body height. The left foot (or the right foot of a left-hander) should step directly toward home plate, moving to the side six inches or less.
3. In the delivery, the back rotation of the shoulder should not be greater than 165 to 180 degrees. The elbow should be flexed between 70 and 115 degrees.
4. In the follow-through, a smooth, extended motion should slow down the pitching arm gradually. The throwing shoulder should be aligned over the opposite knee after the release of the ball. The upper body should be slightly flexed.

HOW IS THE CURVE BALL THROWN?

The most common effect of spin in sports is something that many people do not believe exists—the curve ball in baseball. You can still find some people who think that the curve ball is just an optical illusion.

The argument of whether a baseball can curve went on for so many years that scientists finally got into the act. A long strip of lightweight tape was attached to a baseball. Then a major league pitcher was asked to throw a curve ball. This is usually done by gripping the ball with the thumb and first two fingers only, with the inside of the thumb pressed against one of the seams of the ball. The ball is then released with a sharp outward snap of the wrist. And the friction between the ball and the thumb and fingers starts it spinning as it heads toward the plate.

After the ball was thrown, the number of twists in the tape was counted. This gave the scientists the number of complete spins the ball had made. The ball was placed in a wind tunnel and spun at the same rate. The results indicated that it is possible to make a ball curve as much as 18 inches away from a straight line within a distance of 60 feet, six inches—the official distance from the pitcher's

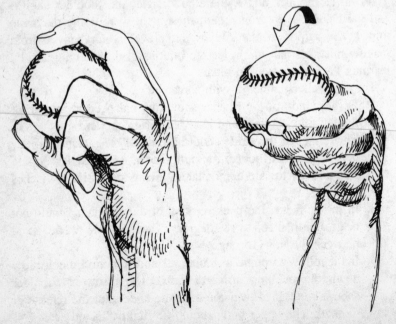

mound to the plate. But the ball must be traveling about 100 feet per second and spinning at a rate of 1,800 revolutions per minute.

Here is what happens: Any thrown object meets air resistance, almost as if there were a wall of air rushing to resist it. But the spinning ball changes this solid wall of air.

Suppose that it is thrown by a right-handed, side-arm pitcher. The spinning ball pulls air around it, but the pressure is increased on the right side (toward third base) and decreased on the left (toward first base). It is spinning counterclockwise, in the same direction that a base runner runs around the bases.

The increased pressure on the right side runs into the wall of air that has piled up in front of the ball and causes the ball to veer to the left. The ball is following the path of least resistance, as the air pressure is lower on the left side. By the way, a curve ball thrown by a side-arm left-hander would curve in the opposite direction, since the ball is spinning clockwise.

HOW IS THE KNUCKLE BALL THROWN?

The knuckle ball, too, depends on air resistance. It is a tricky pitch, and most catchers hate to be part of the battery with a knuckle ball pitcher. You never know where it is going—toward the dugout, toward the batter—moving erratically up, down, or sideways as much as 11 inches. The reasons for this are the seams on the baseball and the pitch's slow rotation of as little as a half-spin between the mound and the plate. That's against the typical fast ball's eight-time rotation.

The ball is held with the index and middle fingers (and the nails) digging into the ball just behind the seam's loop, with the other two fingers on the side of the ball and the thumb along the side of the under seam. The drag is greater on the smooth, unstitched part of the ball, and the ball gets a deflecting push from the smooth side toward the stitched side. As the stitches rotate, the force changes direction. The less spin, the more deflection.

HOW DOES A BAT WORK?

One of the common simple machines used in baseball is really a lever—it's the bat. A lever is only a stiff bar arranged to turn around some fixed point. The bar does not even have to be straight. The fixed point is called the *fulcrum*. The function of the lever is to change the position of a load by applying a force. In the case of the baseball bat, the fulcrum is at the small end, the force is at the point where you grip the bat, and the load is where the ball strikes the bat.

A lot of people argue about what is the best bat. There are those who stick with the old-fashioned wooden bat (including the professional leagues), and those who opt for the aluminum type. And others think the only difference is the sound the bat makes when it hits the ball.

But mechanical engineering students at Tufts University in Medford, Massachusetts, decided to do some investigating in 1991. They used a bat that weighed 32 ounces, had a diameter of 2¾ inches (a quarter inch thicker than standard wood and aluminum bats), and was made of materials that included wood, glass-fiber composites, resins, and fabrics. It supposedly responded like a hardwood bat and had the durability of an aluminum bat.

Developed by Steven Baum of Traverse City, Michigan, it was tested on the Tufts campus by the baseball team (only in practice), and the Boston Red Sox and Detroit Tigers used it in spring training. The idea was to market the bat first to minor league teams, since wood bats have such a long tradition in the major leagues.

One of the Tufts players claimed that it had a bigger "sweet spot" than the usual bat. But he pointed out that it stung more than an aluminum bat if he didn't hit the ball on that sweet spot.

WHAT MAKES A PLAYER A GOOD HOME-RUN HITTER?

Everyone loves a home-run hitter, and a study was made on several home-run hitters some years ago. You might guess that they had more going for them than mere strength. James L. Breen, the head of the Department of Physical Education at Tulane University, found that there were mechanical traits that great home-run hitters had in common. He came up with his list by studying hundreds of major league batters and thousands of feet of motion picture film. Finally, he concentrated on six of the leading home-run hitters of the late 1960s. They were Stan Musial (Cardinals), Ernie Banks

(Cubs), Hank Aaron (Braves), Willie Mays (Giants), Ted Williams (Red Sox), and Mickey Mantle (Yankees).

Breen's list of mechanical traits was made up of four items. First, the center of gravity of the player followed a level plane throughout the swing. (The center of gravity of a body is that point in the object at which the mass is evenly distributed in all directions.) The second point was that from his stance, the batter was able to adjust his head from pitch to pitch. Next, the length of stride was the same on all pitches. And after contact with the ball, the upper-body position was in the same general direction as the flight of the ball.

Breen also found that if the body is kept level at the center of gravity, the bat will be swung in a level path. This is the most effective kind of swing. Having the proper head position lets the batter

watch the pitch for the longest amount of time. This is especially important when the pitch is a breaking ball, such as a curve or a sinking fast ball. The longer the batter follows the pitch with his eyes, the better able he will be to see the point at which the pitch breaks. Also, the batter, by holding his head properly, can reduce the angle at which he sees the ball—that means he will see it more clearly.

If the batter keeps his arms straight when he is swinging, he can bring the bat around much faster than if his arms are bent. Hitters who bend their arms tend to pull the handle of the bat around as they swing. That messes up the lever action of the bat.

Quicker bat speed, along with the ability to watch the ball for the longest period of time, helps the batter to judge more accurately where the ball will be when it is hit. The average batter, looking at a pitch that is traveling 80 miles per hour, has to start his swing when the ball is about 33 feet from the plate. The home-run hitters in this study were able to wait until the ball was only 24 feet from the plate.

The speed of the swing from the time the bat was swung until contact was made varied in this group of hitters. Musial's time was 0.19 seconds and Williams' time was 0.23 seconds. An average hitter's speed would be about 0.28 seconds.

Each of these hitters, although their batting stances were different, took the same straightforward stride as he swung. And each had a similar follow-through motion. As the bat was swung, they pushed off on the back foot, putting all of their force in one direction. Their weight was taken off the back foot when contact was made with the ball, which shifted the center of gravity of their bodies in the direction of the ball. Poorer hitters often shift their centers of gravity backward by putting their weight on the back foot. This results in a loss of power. Gravity, stride, straight arms, head position—whatever these men were doing, they obviously were doing it right.

MORE ON THE SCIENCE OF BATTING

You can forget your thinking caps. Baseball, with its many strategies, is often thought of as being a thinking person's game. But it may be that the smartest hitters leave their brains in the dugout. Yogi Berra's statement that he couldn't think while he hit might have been one of the smartest things that that baseball analyst ever said.

Tom Hanson, a baseball coach at Skidmore College, wrote his doctoral dissertation on the thinking hitter. He claimed that batters simply have no time to think during the four-tenths of a second it takes a good fast ball to go from the pitcher's hand to the catcher's mitt. Hanson contended: "If you are thinking, you are in trouble. Information should go from your eyes to your hands and bypass the brain." The best hitters, he found, are the most relaxed hitters. "The key is not to get tense and anxious. That tightens the muscles and a tight muscle is a slow muscle."

And Judson Berkey, a senior at Thomas Jefferson High School

for Science and Technology, designed a computer model in 1991 to simulate the flight of a baseball. He had come across a study by scientists at Tulane University that assumed that the spin of the ball does not decrease as it travels through the air. That didn't make sense to Berkey, who pointed out that "the ball doesn't come down whizzing through the air. It's coming down pretty soft."

From his computer work, he theorized that to launch a ball the furthest, a batter should connect with the ball at an angle between 32 and 40 degrees from the horizontal and apply as much backspin as possible.

As he said, and you might have to go to a physics teacher to get this translated: "Previous research stated that the verticle launch angle of the baseball from a baseball bat that maximizes the distance the ball travels decreases considerably as the magnitude of the spin increases. These results, however, neglected two aspects of a baseball in flight. They neglected to consider the variation of the coefficient of drag with the velocity of the baseball and the spin reduction due to the torque that is produced by the spin of the baseball."

Finally, Dr. Paul Lagace of the Massachusetts Institute of Technology noticed something after the roof behind home plate in Boston's Fenway Park was torn down following the 1988 season and replaced with a higher one. Balls that once soared into the stands were falling short.

He had his students in his aeronautics and astronautics courses build a wooden model of the ballpark. The model was then put in a wind tunnel for tests. He found that the higher stands created a vortex, or backwind, that could cause a fly ball hit to center field travel about ten feet less.

ON WHICH SIDE OF THE PLATE SHOULD A BATTER STAND?

It may be true that most batters—and that includes the batters in the big leagues—stand on the wrong side of the plate. Forgetting all about good switch hitters, who are in a class by themselves, it seems normal to stand on the left side of the plate, if you are right-handed, and on the right side, if you are left-handed. Right-handers have stronger muscles on the right side of their bodies, and left-handers are stronger on the left. That puts the strong side in a position to drive the bat across the plate.

But the problem is that if the batter isn't hitting the ball, the most powerful swing in the world won't build up his or her batting average. The problem is in the eyes, not the muslces. Everyone is either right-eyed or left-eyed, with one eye being dominant over the other. You can test which of your eyes is dominant. With both eyes open, hold up a pencil, or some other straight object (your finger will do). Now use the tip of the pencil as a back sight on a rifle, and line it up with a point (say the corner of a door) on the opposite side of the room. Use this point as a front sight. Now, holding the pencil steady, close your left eye. If the pencil and the door corner are still lined up, you are right-eyed. Now open your left eye and close your right. The pencil tip should now move to the right, showing that it is the recessive eye. If you are left-eyed, the results will be the opposite.

Now, chances are that you are right-eyed if you are right-handed, and left-eyed if you are left-handed. But there are a few people who are known as cross-dominants—right-handers who are left-eyed and left-handers who are right-eyed.

So here's the problem. Most people, standing on the traditional side of the plate, are standing so that their dominant eye is farthest from the ball. That makes it more difficult to make contact. But is this serious?

Two studies indicate that is is. Dr. Jose M. Portal of the University of Florida College of Medicine studied 23 members of the university baseball team in 1988, and Dr. Donald Tieg studied 400 major leaguers in 1980. Both found that the players with the highest batting averages were cross-dominants. These were the men who swung with their most powerful muscles and still had the dominant eye nearest the ball. It turns out that only five percent of right-handed people are cross-dominant, but almost half of the left-handers (who constitute only about ten percent of the population) are cross-dominant.

Maybe all of us should consider batting from the side of the plate where our dominant eye is nearest the pitcher. It may seem awkward at first, and we possibly won't have as much power, but we should get more contact with the ball.

Index